103946

Sterkx

Partners in rebellion

Date Due

JAN 19 '83			
OCT 2 8 1990			
NOV 0 9 1990			
NOV 27 1990			
DEC 1 8 1990			
MAY 2 '95			
OCT 2 4 2005			

**CHABOT
COLLEGE
LIBRARY**

25555 Hesperian Boulevard
Hayward, CA 94545

Partners in Rebellion:

ALABAMA WOMEN IN THE CIVIL WAR

Also by H. E. Sterkx

Some Notable Alabama Women
During the Civil War

Partners in Rebellion:

ALABAMA WOMEN IN THE CIVIL WAR

H. E. Sterkx

Rutherford • *Madison* • *Teaneck*
Fairleigh Dickinson University Press

© 1970 by Associated University Presses, Inc.
Library of Congress Catalogue Card Number: 74-99326

Associated University Presses, Inc.
Cranbury, New Jersey 08512

ISBN: 0-8386-7614-6
Printed in the United States of America

The author wishes to thank Bell I. Wiley and Atheneum Publishers
for permission to quote from Bell Irvin Wiley, *The Road to
Appomattox*. Copyright © 1956 by Memphis State College Press.
Reprinted by permission of Atheneum Publishers.

For
HATTIE DAVIS STERKX

Contents

Contents

Preface

The history of the Civil War is a familiar one nowadays, almost too familiar; its undoubted drama and significance for Americans have been dulled by repetition. For over a century both amateur and professional historians have produced an endless stream of studies covering nearly every aspect of that celebrated conflict. Its causes and effects have been thoroughly examined, countless theses expounded, attacked, and subjected to revision time and again. Innumerable debates have raged over the merits and demerits of its battles and leaders, the roles of the ordinary soldier, the plain folk, the aristocracy, and the slaves—even hay and salt have come under scrutiny as significant factors in determining the outcome. It has aroused the interest of Hollywood film-makers and supplies the theme of several television series. From 1961 to 1965 Americans staged four years of pageants, round-table discussion groups, and other projects commemorating the centennial of the Civil War. Indeed, it would appear that there is nothing left unwritten or done about the War Between the States, and yet much remains to be said about the role of women during wartime.

Until recently the academic world, and that but rarely and exiguously, has taken little notice of the women's role that was such a vivid part of the time and had so great an impact on it. Among the notable exceptions are the generation-old work of Francis B. Simkins and James M.

Patton on Confederate women, and the more recent comprehensive study of women on both sides of the line by Mary Elizabeth Massey. These competent scholars have contributed much toward the preparation of my study of Alabama women in the Confederacy and at the same time made it exceedingly difficult to follow them. I have been constantly aware of their high standards of writing and that it would be necessary for me to cover some of the same material already published. There were times in which I considered abandoning the project and concentrating my energies in teaching and in attending college committee meetings regularly, but I persisted with the hope that what I have found may throw additional light on a neglected population in one of the Confederate States.

When beginning the research in 1963 I must confess having had the preconceived notion of producing a burlesque of Alabama's Confederate women. At that time there seemed to be no other way of presenting the activities of what I thought to be a body of helpless, mostly ornamental little creatures who spent their time preparing for military balls, and who occasionally nursed wounded soldiers. To be sure, many fell into this category, but as the work progressed the force of evidence revealed that the majority were responsible for far more wartime activities and I could not stop admiring these for their devotion to duty as they saw it. In writing this book I have tried to recreate the role of over 130,000 white Confederate sympathizers between the ages of fifteen through sixty. Regrettably, there is little concerning the role of slave women except that which was viewed through the eyes of whites. The vast majority were illiterate and left no substantial amount of records of their feelings about matters during four years of conflict. It is necessarily the white women's story, and I have acted primarily as their reporter, supplying the organization and necessary prepositions and conjunctions between quotations.

There is no intent to resurrect the past for its own sweet, sentimental sake. War is seldom sweet or sentimental, but is nearly always traumatic for the generation that experiences it, and for those who come after. Also, considerable effort has been made to avoid lauding or debunking any one person or any one class of women involved in the war. When such appears, it is the product of the extant evidence rather than an exposé or a play for sensationalism.

It has been difficult to reach general conclusions of the impact of war on a cast of thousands. Each woman's reaction was naturally conditioned by her own personal considerations, past experiences, and the environment in which she lived. If there is any common denominator among them it was the conviction that all great enterprises were easy and did not necessarily need careful planning, preparation, organization, and the collaboration of competent and well-trained personnel. This, of course, their male compatriots were also inclined to believe. They seemed to think that all that was needed for victory was enthusiasm, self-sacrifice, volunteers heroically ready to die, and a great and fearless leader showing the way. Enemy forces would vanish, stupendous problems would solve themselves as if by magic, as long as one had faith in the cause and in its ultimate success. But it did not turn out that way. It was not a success story, but one thing is certain: matters would surely have gone far worse without the help of feminine noncombatants.

It is my pleasure to acknowledge a debt of gratitude to many individuals who have contributed in various ways to the preparation of this work. Among these are: the staffs of the Alabama Department of Archives and History; the Duke University Manuscript Division; the Southern Historical Collection of the University of North Carolina; Emory University Library; the Georgia Department of Archives and History; the Amelia Gayle Gorgas Library of the University of Alabama; the Library of Congress; and the National Archives. In particular I am in the debt of Mr. Milo B. Howard, Jr., Director of the Alabama Department of Archives and History, for his sage advice and valuable assistance in reading and criticizing the manuscript. Thanks are due to Mrs. Virginia K. Jones, Mrs. Jessie Cobb, Mrs. Alma Pate, and Mr. William Letford of the Archives staff for their tireless efforts in helping me to locate the great number of manuscripts and newspapers used in the book. I give grateful acknowledgment to Mrs. Frances Clarke for her expert reproduction of illustrations. Finally, I am under heavy obligation to Professor Brooks Thompson of Troy State University for his support and encouragement, and to his wife, Harriett, for her ungrudging assistance in typing the finished product.

Acknowledgments

The author wishes to thank the following for their kind permission to quote from copyrighted material:

Bobbs-Merrill Company, Inc., for permission to quote from Bell I. Wiley, *The Life of Johnny Reb: The Common Soldier in the Confederacy*. Copyright © 1943 by the Bobbs-Merrill Company, Inc.

Harvey S. Ford, for permission to quote from Harvey S. Ford, ed., *John Beatty, The Citizen Soldier or, Memoirs of a Volunteer*, W. W. Norton & Company, 1946. Copyright © 1946 by Harvey S. Ford.

Harper & Row, Publishers, Incorporated, for permission to quote from John A. Wyeth, *That Devil Forrest: Life of General Nathan Bedford Forrest*. Copyright © 1959 by Harper & Row, Publishers, Incorporated.

Houghton Mifflin Company, for permission to quote from Ben Ames Williams, ed., *Mary Boykin Chestnut, A Diary from Dixie*. Copyright © 1949 by Houghton Mifflin Company.

Alfred A. Knopf, Inc., for permission to quote from Mary Elizabeth Massey, *Bonnet Brigades*. Copyright © 1966 by Alfred A. Knopf, Inc.

Louisiana State University Press, for permission to quote from Richard B. Harwell, ed., *Kate: The Journal of a Confederate Nurse*. Copyright © 1959 by Louisiana State University Press.

University of Alabama Press, for permission to quote

Partners in Rebellion:

ALABAMA WOMEN IN THE CIVIL WAR

Chabot
College

1

Disunion, disunion is the watchword everywhere. . . . Men seem drunk with passion, and
women share their frenzy.

It was good to be a free white man in nineteenth century
America. In countless ways before the Civil War he
was the master sex—infinitely freer than women in his
movements, choice of occupation, and educational opportunities. Patriarchal authority gave him an exclusive monopoly of political affairs, and men occupied every level of
government from county clerk to the high office of the
president. It was almost always a male who labored or
directed work in the fields and factories, preached the
gospel, practiced the professions, and when physical danger threatened, the "weaker sex" looked to him for protection. More often than not, there was a woman in every
man's life, but whether she was a wife or dependent relative he expected her to remain in the background. It had
always been this way. Man-made custom inherited from
European ancestors had long decreed that woman's special place was in the home and that she should leave the
outside world to males.

Yet there were signs of discontent. Women of the urban
and industrial northeastern areas were becoming better
educated, more economically independent, and less satisfied

with second-class citizenship. It was here that a few had "leaped from their spheres," and had begun demanding equal rights with "the lords of creation."[1] The vast majority everywhere, however, were content with their lot. They just wanted to meet a "nice boy," get married, and provide a good home for their husband and children.

An antebellum Alabama girl could not have agreed more with this point of view. Aside from personal inclination, she was trained from childhood to prepare herself for marriage and motherhood. It was universally recognized as her "duty" and, according to Benjamin Fickling Porter, the Alabama legislator responsible for the 1839 law permitting married women to own property separately from husbands, "The most miserable thing in nature . . . except an old bachelor . . . is an old maid."[2] Even if she had wanted to strike out alone, or was forced into becoming a breadwinner, there were almost insurmountable obstacles in the way. For one thing, public opinion frowned on work for women outside of the home, but if these prejudices did not matter, there was still the problem of securing remunerative employment. Alabama's preoccupation with agriculture left little capital for industrial development and by 1860 there were only 1,097 women employed in industrial work of all kinds compared to 6,792 male wage earners. Most of these were unskilled laborers in such light industries as textiles, clothing, and shoemaking.[3]

Opportunities to engage in business for themselves were even more limited than industrial work. Potential businesswomen not only encountered strong public hostility, but they also faced the task of securing sufficient capital for initiating business enterprises. Despite these handicaps a few operated small millinery shops with money they had

inherited or borrowed from relatives. The largest number
of these stores was concentrated in the two urban centers
of Mobile and Montgomery, but nearly every county-seat
town had at least one during the antebellum period. Typical was the "Tuskegee Millinery Establishment" of a Mrs.
Wolff, who offered local patrons an impressive array of
fancy goods consisting of Irish linens, ivory fans, picnic
gloves, hoop skirts of from four to thirty springs, and
a large assortment of perfumes and costume jewelry.[4]
Others became managers of rooming houses, seamstresses,
and proprietors of peripatetic dancing schools.

The greatest professional opportunity open to women
was in school teaching, but here, too, they encountered
difficulties. The state did not establish a public school system until 1854, and even then men were given priority as
teachers. Only those women in dire need would seek work
in state schools, for in 1857 the superintendent of education found nineteen out of twenty school buildings in an
unfinished condition, "without chimneys or stoves, either
unceiled or unplastered, badly ventilated or entirely without windows. . . ." An ever-increasing number, however,
found teaching positions in private academies. By 1860
there were 206 such institutions in existence, with an aver-
age of two instructors each and usually operated by a man
and his wife.[5]

Some of these were owned exclusively by women and
for the most part consisted of fashionable finishing schools
catering to the children of the elite. In every case, whether
the institution was an academy or bore the more ambitious
name of college, the curriculum emphasized preparation
for marriage and how to become a lady.

A considerable number of educated women chose writing as a career, but only a handful derived an income from

their works or received any kind of recognition for literary talent beyond the state of Alabama. An exception was Caroline Lee Hentz, the Massachusetts-born teacher and a prolific writer of romantic fiction, who extolled the virtues of Southern life and manners. In her novel, *The Planter's Northern Bride,* the hero emerges as the strong Victorian *pater familias* who succeeds in convincing his abolitionist-wife that she should accept the righteousness of slavery. Augusta Jane Evans, the best-selling Southern novelist of the prewar period, also wrote to perpetuate women's place in American society. In *Beulah* she assailed those women who were in the process of rejecting their traditional role and asked for God's help in leading them "back to the hearthstone, that holy-post, which too many, alas, have deserted."[6]

It is not surprising that the overwhelming majority of Alabama women did not torment themselves about the lack of equality with their menfolk. Anonymity and partial seclusion had their compensations in giving more time for domestic duties or just being a "lady." Undoubtedly many felt that open rebellion might result in uprooting the foundations supporting the chivalric ideal, which held that woman was made of finer stuff than man, was someone to be admired, adored, and protected from the crudities of the world.[7] Life under these standards offered too many safeguards against male tyranny to risk disrupting the *status quo,* and, consequently, no women's rights movement materialized in Alabama. Besides, as conservative Southerners thoroughly steeped in the traditions of slavery, they had sound reasons for regarding Northern feminists as mere auxiliaries to the abolition movement. Further, few relished the idea of giving aid and comfort to any organization whose aims included the destruction of the slave system.

For three decades nearly all antebellum Alabamians came to accept the myriad arguments in defense of slavery as unassailable truths. It became a highly moral institution and a "positive good" in all of its forms; abolitionists, therefore, were nothing more than dangerous fanatics bent on destroying the most important element supporting their way of life. Even those of both sexes personally unfamiliar with exact details of the issues involved had learned through informal sources to be wary of any critic of the peculiar institution. Prior to the war the well-known orator William Lowndes Yancey made hundreds of speeches damning the opponents of slavery and prescribing states' rights as the only protection left Southerners against the growing Northern anti-slavery forces.[8]

As one sectional crisis followed another in quick succession, other partisans took to the speakers' stands and the pulpit, and intense authors issued inflammatory broadsides in books and in the press. Many of the state's editors attacked abolitionists in the most scurrilous language. Subscribers were constantly reminded to be on the lookout for secret agents spreading dissension among the slave population. A quite typical example of this kind of journalism appeared in September of 1860 when several papers carried a story describing how an alert group of citizens aboard a ship at New Orleans had discovered an abolitionist disguised in female dress. According to the report "a queer looking woman" had been conducting herself in a suspicious manner for several days and when a delegation of passengers attempted to ascertain "her" intentions the truth came out. Evidence was produced which purported to show that the agent in question had already "spread devastation" among Texas slaves and had plans to continue doing the same in other Gulf states. However, before the police arrived the "abolitionist in crinoline" escaped, and ostensibly beat a hasty retreat "to a more congenial climate."[9]

Slavery apologists succeeded in winning over a considerable body of articulate women to consider abolitionists, and finally every Northerner, as the malevolent incarnation of evil. This hard core of women stood ready to defend Southern institutions at every turn, but at no time did the women flout established custom by joining the men on public platforms in condemning the "common enemy." On the other hand, scores of concerned females waged an unrelenting campaign of hate for these "villains" in their diaries, letters, and at gossip sessions. From the written sources it becomes evident that their views paralleled those of the men and in a few rare cases they were far more severe in their condemnation. To some the very word "abolitionist" carried the connotation of bugbear and was used to frighten naughty children or to cast aspersions upon enemies and rivals. In 1855 Mrs. E. P. Lee of Uniontown applied the word in this sense when she wrote to her sister, branding members of the Know-Nothing party as "real abolitionists, every hoof of them traitors to their country," simply because their very existence might endanger the election of states' rights democrats.[10]

When the leaders of the anti-slavery societies accelerated their campaign during the late 1850s, Alabama was swept with wild rumors of impending slave insurrections until the situation reached near-panic conditions. In some remote rural areas terrified women began looking upon every stranger as a possible abolitionist. Sarah Espy, the

busy owner of a Cherokee County plantation, was typical
of those who were only too ready to believe the worst of
rumors. She was convinced that her community was literally teeming with abolitionists going about committing
every kind of crime and mischief. According to her diary,
they had burned a neighbor's barn, induced his slaves to
run away, and she expected that her property would be
next. John Brown's 1859 raid on Harper's Ferry intensified her fears, but on learning of his execution she expressed the hope that "peace attend, and follow, and may
the women and children of the South be saved from their
Northern Murderers." But Sarah's apprehensions never
completely subsided, and as the 1860 presidential campaign drew near she predicted that only John Brecken-
ridge's election could save the nation from disaster.[11]

The strongest opposition to abolitionism originated in
the rich Black Belt counties of south and central Alabama.
In this streak of fertile soil lived large plantation owners
known as "cotton snobs"—the new rich—who zealously
guarded their social, economic, and political hegemony
against any contestant. Here, a few bolder spirits who
wished to be more than mere spectators in the sectional
struggle wrote letters to newspapers expressing their personal opinions on the issue. Still fewer of them submitted
plans, which they guaranteed would bring an end to the
Northern movement.

One of the most publicized plans came from an anony-
mous woman of Lowndes County who identified herself
only as "Lowndes Matron." On January 28, 1860, she
began a series of letters which, continued over three
months in the pro-secession *Montgomery Mail*, outlined
a scheme that she thought a unique solution. In language
reminiscent of a latter-day suffragette, this matron opened

with a blast against "the lords of the earth" for doing nothing but "talking a great deal and making thundering speeches about abolitionists wrongs." Since such efforts had already proved ineffective, she proposed that all housewives form themselves into associations to lay plans for effecting a boycott against Northern manufactured goods. No serious inconvenience was anticipated, because it was a simple matter of buying the necessities of life that were made in the South or in foreign countries. All Southern women were invited to participate and at the same time stage a buyers' strike against local merchants who refused "to assist us in carrying out this enterprise."[12]

In a short time the boycott idea attracted enough support so that the women began to organize. At the first meeting they adopted the name of "Lowndes Ladies for the South," elected a slate of officers, and wrote a constitution. In a most formal manner, this group adopted resolutions indicting not only anti-slavery societies, but all Northern people for advocating the equality of the races. They wanted the world to know that "if such equality became a reality, it would result in religious, moral, and political degradation and would fall alike upon all who could not flee from the country." They protested that they had always been loyal citizens, but in light of Northern hostility it seemed to them "strange! yea, passing strange! that ere long our destruction is sure, if not averted by the individual exertions of ourselves to save the country." This could be done by simply "annoying and crippling the energies of the common enemy" through the establishment of an absolute boycott.[13]

Other Black Belt women imitated the Lowndes group and after several days of concerted action boasted that they had "put local merchants on the right track." The legislature, too, responded with a resolution calling for the immediate end of commercial intercourse between Alabama and the Northern states. All citizens were urged to form organizations whose members would agree to patronize only Southern or foreign-made products.[14] The "Lowndes Matron's" reaction to this action was considerably less than enthusiastic. It appeared to her that the lawmakers were woefully remiss in their duty as Southerners for not imposing stronger legislation against local merchants who still refused to cooperate. In a letter addressed to the General Assembly, she demanded drastic measures, and, if such were not forthcoming, then the legislators themselves were challenged to "take off your coats, roll up your sleeves and go to work to produce cotton gins, textiles, carpets, and other household luxuries."[15]

Another member of the Lowndes group who wrote under the name of "A True Southern Woman" echoed these suggestions, but went on to denounce those Alabama women who had married Yankees and who were sending their children to mixed schools in the North. Such liaisons were accounted unpatriotic and ought to be discouraged or prohibited altogether in the future. The proposed ban on intersectional marriages was too extreme for the editors of the paper, who had acted as the boycotters' mentors and publicists from the beginning of the project. After complimenting the Lowndes women for outstanding work in inciting "their fathers, brothers, and sons to stand resolutely for Southern Rights," they informed the "True Southern Woman" that she was out of line. In no uncertain words they let her know that many Northerners living in the state were more loyal than all too many native-born Southerners of their acquaintance.[16]

Not all sections of the state acquiesced in the leadership
of the Black Belt. No parts were more recalcitrant than
the piney woods uplands of Alabama, where small and
slaveless farmers tilled poor soils for a meager livelihood.
These fiercely independent "plain folk" had little in common with the masters of the great plantations and tended
to regard them with mistrust or even hostility. Equally
recalcitrant was the Tennessee River Valley area located
in north Alabama, the homeland of wealthy planters who
looked upon abolitionists with no less animosity than their
counterparts in the southern counties. Yet, it should be
noted that the existence of an intra-state political struggle
of long standing with the Black Belt constrained them
from accepting any leadership from that quarter. Even
during the secession crisis both northern planters and their
hillbilly neighbors held firmly to unionist principles until
forced to yield to the numerical power of the southern
secessionists.[17]

Consequently, the matter of boycotting Northern goods
failed to attract large numbers of women in this area.
However, a small group from Tuscumbia, acting in an
independent capacity, formed such an association just a
short time before the state left the Union. Early in January of 1861 its members approved a simple resolution,
without comment, not to buy anything made "north of
the Mason and Dixon Line" after January 16, 1861.
Sensing that secession would have become an accomplished
fact by that date, they felt it their duty "to comfort and
help our husbands, brothers and young men to the utmost"
in case of war.[18]

The secession movement, on the other hand, received
strong endorsement from Black Belt women. Suspension
of commercial relations with the free states proved to be

the thinnest kind of disguise in aiding in the campaign to carry Alabama out of the Union. Almost immediately after the "Lowndes Ladies for the South" began operation, its garrulous leader urged independence as the best guarantee for maintaining white supremacy. In one of her anti-Yankee blasts published on March 8, 1860, "Lowndes Matron" threw aside all pretense by pleading with Alabamians "to strike for independence . . . or amalgamate."[19] After Lincoln's election her writings took on stronger dimensions. She argued that there was now no alternative except to get out or to face certain annihilation. In an effort to win over moderates, this female fire-eater blithely dismissed the idea that such a step might result in war since she was of the opinion that Northerners possessed no will to fight. As if depicting a vision of an impregnable, independent Southern utopia, she justified her stand on the grounds that

> Yankee hirelings cannot look honest-hearted Southerners in the face very long, especially when we feel our position to them is that of David and Goliath; and when there are so many noble hearted women to utter fervently what Saul said to David, 'Go, and the Lord be with thee'.[20]

The Republican victory had an electrifying effect upon scores of south Alabama women. Female wile and ingenuity in all their forms were brought into play in advancing the one all-consuming goal of leaving the Union. A Montgomery sewing circle began making blue cockades for men's hat as a symbol that the wearer favored secession. The members also offered to supply enough badges for every male citizen so that there could be no excuse for not wearing them.[21] A similar project was undertaken in

Eufaula. Here the sewing-circle members stationed themselves on street corners and began distributing cockades to male pedestrians. It was reported that only one man had refused a badge because he was opposed to secession. This unexpected response so infuriated the donor that she turned to a gathering crowd and denounced the man as a coward. Among other things, she commanded the men present "to protect that man's wife and children, should the South have to resort to arms in defense of its rights."[22] Shortly before this incident, the same group of ladies had become so highly enraged on learning that a pro-Union meeting at Florence had condemned a local military tax measure that they offered to pay the money themselves. They also voted to send a hoop skirt to the chairman as a mark of his cowardice.[23]

Many others demonstrated their feelings by making flags containing strong pro-secession mottoes. On December 18, 1860, the Mobile women's auxiliary of the "Young Men's Secession Association" staged a gala affair of dancing and dining at the Odd Fellows Hall, after which they presented a banner, emblazoned with "Alabama the Time Has Come,"[24] to the members of the Association. Less ingenious females promoted secession through bursts of bravado at social affairs. Such was the case of a young girl of Montgomery who had sat silently through several hours of conversation about the prospects of a Republican victory at an 1859 New Year's Eve party. Unable to contain her pent-up feelings any longer, she suddenly arose from her chair and, "stamping her foot . . . with the air of a heroine worthy of a Maid of Orleans," proceeded to let the revelers know that she was willing "to put on a uniform and shoulder a musket . . . for the rights and honor of the South."[25]

With less bombast, another New Year celebrant at Tuskegee in 1861 became so excited about secession talk that she left the party and wrote her brother in New Orleans to come home immediately because "your country may need you . . . ere long. . . ."[26] Indeed, even poetry was marshalled into the cause of separation. Julia L. Keyes composed a fifteen-stanza work entitled, "We'll Divide It, Tho' We Perish." A sample of her argument ran thus:

> We'll divide it though the foe men
> Should come, with torch and guns,
> Our loved and loving women
> Are arming Southern sons.[27]

Female secessionists from other Southern states pressed their Alabama sisters to demand action. For example, one living in Louisiana wrote to her son in Montgomery on November 28, 1860, asking what Alabama intended doing in view of Lincoln's election. For her part, she "had rather die than live under the administration of a Black Republican," and hoped that her native state would not delay in seceding so that she might return home in case Louisiana elected to remain in the United States.[28] A South Carolina woman described the wonderful effects secession had had on the men of that state. In her words, it was "a tonic for the males since the old men seem to be rejuvenated and the young men . . . ready . . . to sacrifice their life's blood in the cause." She went on to guarantee the same therapeutic effects for Alabama if the women would only arouse the men into taking action. She closed with the explanation that it was impossible for her to visit Alabama in order to point out further advantages because as matters then stood it would require her to travel in the

United States and that was the last thing she wanted to do.[29]

After the men carried Alabama out of the Union on January 11, 1861, many who had favored secession were suddenly seized with mixed emotions. Kate Cumming of Mobile was saddened when she learned "what we had done . . . not from any wrong or unlawfulness, but from the fact that, united, we were stronger than we would be separated; and I also feared the bloodshed which might ensue." The future hospital matron, however, had second thoughts and rejoiced over secession as the only possible solution because "no happiness can exist in a union without concord; and there can be no concord . . . where any two people are so diametrically opposed to each other" as the Northern and Southern states.[30]

A similar reaction gripped Virginia Clay, but for different reasons. As a senator's wife, and one of the leading hostesses of antebellum Washington, she was in a strategic position to assess the situation as it developed in the nation's capital. Even though her sympathies were unquestionably pro-Southern, she was incapable of hate and was never an ardent secessionist. Yet, when her husband resigned his senate seat and they prepared to return home, the seriousness of the situation hit Virginia hard. It was a doleful scene for the self-styled "Belle of the Fifties." "Each step," she wrote, "in preparation to leave was a pang," since it meant that many "farewells . . . we knew, would be final."[31] In reality it marked the end of her social reign and the starting of a new and uncertain career in a future Confederate capital.

On the other hand, there were those who expressed unmitigated joy. It was the realization of a long-sought-for goal to Augusta Jane Evans of Mobile. Just two days after Alabama seceded, she wrote to a friend proclaiming herself as always having been "an earnest and uncompromising Secessionist." "As a citizen of Alabama," she continued, "I am proud . . . we have irrevocably linked our destiny with the Carolinas, and if necessary will *drain our veins* rather than yield to the ignominious rule of Black Republicanism. . . ."[32] Unqualified approval came from a few of the Northern-born female residents of the state. Speaking with the zeal of converts or out of a sense of survival, these adopted Southerners made quite a case in justifying secession. Ellen Noyes Jackson was one, at least, who took this line of thought when she wrote to her sister in Boston explaining why the Confederacy was demanding all of the forts within its borders. It was her considered opinion that such installations were not erected "to defend Massachusetts or New York" but were established for the protection of the Southern people. They should have been surrendered before March 4, 1861, to prevent the incoming Republican administration from coercing the states back into the Union and thus triggering the start of war.[33]

Support and encouragement came from the most unexpected sources. The press gave full coverage to those pro-Southern Northern women who endorsed secession as part of the campaign to justify what had already been done. A case in point was the letter from a "Lady of Cincinnati," who admitted that she had never been out of Ohio, but since Lincoln's election she wanted to move South. The president-elect was held responsible for "all the confusion and discord that led to the dissolution of our once glorious Union" and she went on to offer her "humble services" to any Southern governor "to assist in guarding magazines, protecting the Capitals, etc."[34] Another outsider, under the soubriquet of "A Lady in Washington," admonished Ala-

bamians to stand firm. If they would do so "in the attitude
of chivalrous and determined people . . . then I say this
attitude commands my unqualified approval."[35]

It took a great deal of courage to contest the wave of
anti-Northern jeremiads, but to advocate moderation, be
it ever so mild, required the soul of a martyr. Yet, there
were a few women, and perhaps many more than the records show, who considered secession unnecessary or even
unconstitutional. The poorly educated Elizsay Bell of
strongly Unionist Winston County regarded her brother's
action in favoring the secession movement as "a hart
rending thing to me," and warned him to "come back
before [you] will be prest back by force." At the same
time Miss Bell gave written notice that she was withdraw-
ing an earlier proposition that her kinsman help find her
a suitable husband. This ardent Unionist proudly announced that she "would disdain to keep company with a
disunionist for if he will cecede from the government . . .
he woud cecede from his family."[36]

By and large those Alabamians who bucked the prevailing opinion kept their counsels in secret, but there was one
dubbed the "Lady Sensationalist," who wrote disapprovingly of a highly charged atmosphere that had come over
the citizens of Wetumpka. Implying that she was a Unionist, she was shocked at seeing the townspeople "sporting
like butterflies on the brink of ruin . . . and every man
dances even with a pistol in his belt and a bowie knife in
his bosom." It was an unreal world in which "men seem
drunk with passion, and women share their frenzy. . . . Disunion, disunion is the watchword everywhere," she observed, and continued, "peacefully if possible, if not, with
bloodshed and ruin as its attendant."[37]

In such an atmosphere, therefore, it was inevitable that

suspicion should fall on those Northerners who had not made public pronouncements concerning their Southern allegiance. Those holding liberal opinions either kept quiet or fled across the border to the North. Veteran school teachers, who are usually well adjusted to criticism from students in less troublesome time, now came under stronger suspicion as sinister characters engaged in deadly plots against the established order. This was especially true of the Yankee-born Sarah Follansbee, who resigned her position at Judson College because of student hostility. Going to Montgomery in 1861 to teach at the "Home School," it was not long before she overheard demeaning rumors about being "that *Yankee* teacher" and other unkind remarks. As if to beard the little lions in their den, she got permission to speak before the student body to explain her neutrality. In a prepared statement she told the assembly that it was her job "to teach you a course of study, not political topics and if I am not welcome or not appreciated I will go where I will be." The explanation was apparently satisfactory and she was able to report that afterwards "kind attention upon kind attention was showered upon me."[38]

Yet, Sarah was slated to experience more serious trouble. Some adults of the capital city thought she constituted a one-woman fifth column of such force that she should be expelled from the town in the interest of public safety. On several occasions a nameless group accused her of sending vital information in coded letters to Northern military authorities. In one particular letter, which had been intercepted, she had casually mentioned owning fifty chickens, having plenty of eggs to eat, and enjoying the company of pleasant friends. These harmless remarks were written to reassure Northern relatives that she was

content with living in the Confederacy, but the fifty chickens were interpreted to mean fifty unionists, "the eggs
something adverse" about the South, and the words
"pleasant friends" misconstrued to mean "plenty of
Northern Sympathizers" under her leadership.

For a time her life was in danger. Sympathetic friends
let her know that a certain man had made the remark that
"he would be glad to see her beautiful curls wound
around the hangman's rope" if the charges were true.
Others made similar threats, but when the affair got out
of control the president of a Baptist College at Tuskegee,
came to her defense by pointing out to her accusers that she
was "the presiding teacher of the children of such men as
our governor, general so and so, Cols. so and so, and the
best citizens of Montgomery are glad to have their daughters under her instruction and care."[39] With this impressive recommendation the matter was dropped, but hardly
forgotten, and Miss Follansbee was treated as an alien
by some for the remainder of the war.

Experiencing somewhat less hostility were Southerners
from nonseceding border states and especially those who
had connections with prominent Northern officials. Among
such as these was Elodie Todd, the ardent Confederate
half-sister of Mrs. Abraham Lincoln and a resident of
Selma during the Civil War period. Even her engagement and later marriage to Confederate Captain Nathaniel H. R. Dawson proved to be no guarantee of immunity
from threatening and slanderous remarks. On July 4,
1861, she was so dispirited over the frequency of reckless
threats aimed against President Lincoln that she wrote
Dawson; "I never go in Public that my feelings are not
wounded . . . for people constantly wish he may be hung
& all such evils may attend his foot steps."[40] Highly sensi-
tive over the failure of her home state of Kentucky to

secede, she would lash out against the gentlest kind of teasing on this score. Once in 1862 she wrote her husband of how "often my spirits flag when I think of home . . . and of myself a stranger in a strange land, unloved, I feel as tho I could bear it no more but I know I am not doing my duty in giving way."[41]

The formation of the Confederacy was men's handiwork, but a few women, feeling that it was their government too, came forward with advice on matters that they deemed important for the politicians to consider. Fearful that no arrangement had been made for Jefferson Davis's inauguration, the "True Southern Woman" of Lowndes County spoke through letters expressing her views of what constituted a proper ceremony. She suggested that such an event should be conducted with "due form and ceremonial style," and, once more, urged policymakers to establish an elaborate code of ceremonial etiquette in all areas of government. In her opinion displays of show and pageantry provided an air of "majesty and dignity" that would command the respect of all citizens. Besides, it would go a long way in preventing "demagogues and agrarians" from seizing control of the government simply because they could not operate in such an atmosphere.[42]

According to several eye-witnesses, the "True Southern Woman" had no reasons to fret about proper ceremonies. At least one, named Mary Gay, found it "a grand Solemn occasion," and was beside herself when she wrote: "Oh! that scene at the capital of Alabama, when Jefferson Davis . . . took the oath of office and pledged undying fidelity to the best interests of his own sunny Southland."[43] Ellen Noyes Jackson considered it "the greatest day in the annals of Montgomery" as she witnessed a group of young women letting go a shower of flowers from a capitol balcony overlooking the president immediately after he took the oath of office. It was no less than the apotheosis of Davis—"a chivalrous Southern agrarian."[44]

There were others motivated by a sincere desire to be of help who made quiet but determined efforts to influence the course of politics. It was for this reason that Louisiana Bradford of Talladega launched a campaign to get Huntsville named the permanent capital of the Confederacy. She wrote several prominent officials for assistance in promoting her project, but finally selected ex-senator Clement C. Clay, Jr. as her chief spokesman because he was from Huntsville and naturally *"the man to stir up the people on the subject."* Clay was advised to proceed with haste because Georgians had Atlanta as a prospect and Tennesseeans were working in behalf of Chattanooga or Nashville. To her, Richmond would be the poorest kind of choice since it was "too near the Border of that land & People of which we desire no part ever to enter our Boundaries." Huntsville was the only ideal place. For one thing, she thought it was accessible to any part of the new nation by way of the Tennessee River, but, most important of all, the Confederate capital ought to be located in one of the "Cotton States," that is to say, in one such as Alabama, which had fought "the first *Battle alone*" for secession while the border state of Virginia remained in the United States. Huntsville filled her formula perfectly and by "right as well as *courtesy* the permanent capital should be located in the North Alabama city."[45]

Clay quickly accepted Mrs. Bradford's challenge and held a series of meetings at Huntsville to promote the capital idea, but when he became ill the project was abandoned.[46] There were far more pressing matters facing Alabamians. Among these was the matter of raising an army to defend the new nation's bid for independence.

2

Arise, grasp your sword and wield your steel, and drive your enemies from the field.

While visiting a United States prisoner-of-war stockade, the wife of a Yankee politician observed a group of young Confederate inmates absorbed in playing the game of marbles. Thinking that some terrible mistake had been made, the woman asked the guide if they were not children imprisoned by mistake. She was promptly assured that they were indeed captured soldiers, and by way of further explanation she was told that "those damned Confederate women, as soon as a boy baby is born down there, take him and put a bottle of milk in one hand and a musket in the other and shove him into the army."[1] This may have been an overdrawn estimate of the Spartan-like qualities of Southern women, but it came near to describing the patriotic zeal of many in Alabama during the early days of the Civil War.

In the beginning patriotism became the prevailing emotion of the day and it affected old and young alike with the determination to do something, almost anything, to help the Confederacy along the road to success. Absolutely nothing seemed too trivial or impossible for the state's women in achieving this lofty goal. Some of them designed flags for the republic, others made banners and delivered

37

presentation speeches for local military units, and there were still many more who dedicated themselves to the tremendous task of encouraging men to enlist in the armed forces. It was a time like no other in the lives of Alabamians because it offered a rare opportunity for homebound females to participate in public affairs. It was also a romantic time, since there were heroes to admire and villains to hate, and it was a time to prove that the Confederacy constituted an invincible nation united against its unrelentingly aggressive foe, the United States of America.

As a new nation the Confederate States needed ornaments and symbols of its sovereignty, and artistically inclined women quickly responded with designs for an official flag. In January of 1861, Mrs. Winston Hunter of Montgomery was driven by the desire to become the Betsy Ross of the Southern Republic when she submitted a blue flag embossed with seven stars, representing the states already out of the union. Adequate space for additional stars was provided for those states that might join in the near future. It was a fashionable piece with silver fringes and festoons of heavy gold tassels hanging from a gold-colored staff. No wonder one capital city editor found it "the most elegant and elaborate banner that has yet made its appearance."[2] Virginia Clay offered an even fancier flag made of red silk with a gold olive wreath in the upper left-hand corner, pierced by a golden spear. The Clay entry, however, was rejected because "it could not be distinguished at a distance" from other standards on battlefields and was too expensive to manufacture in mass quantities.[3]

In March, 1861, Confederate authorities at Montgomery adopted as the official flag a simple tricolor of red,

white, and blue and it was hoisted on the capitol grounds
by Letitia Tyler, a granddaughter of the former president of the United States.[4] Similar ceremonies were performed in every county throughout the state, where all
kinds of material were utilized in making flags. At Gainesville in west Alabama the ladies salvaged the cloth from
an old "Douglas for President" banner and selected the
town's "prettiest miss" to raise it above the county court
house.[5] Frequently, old trunks and attics were raided for
highly prized and sentimental textiles to form part of the
national flag. In Marion Mrs. Sumpter Lea, a sister-in-
law of Governor Sam Houston of Texas, donated her
wedding dress and she was assured that the finished flag
would be borne bravely "to the scenes of bloodshed."[6]

The outbreak of fighting released an even greater out-
pouring of patriotic fervor. In all fifty-two counties,
hundreds of young women volunteered to make standards
for local military companies and eagerly competed with
each other for the honor of delivering the presentation
speeches. On these occasions no objections were raised
against women speaking out in public and many took full
advantage of the opportunity to demonstrate their ora-
torical skills. Every one of them employed the nineteenth-
century patois of serious rhetoric and florid phrases heavy
with appeals to the fundamental Protestant creed of service that was so much a part of their heritage. Typical of
such oratory was a speech rendered by Hassie Anderson
when she admonished the "Brundidge Guards" of Pike
County to:

> Arise, grasp your sword and wield your steel, and drive
> your enemies from the field. Onward, onward, you gal-
> lant band, save us! save our cherished land. Gird on
> your armor, lift your hearts, and God will shield you

from the darts. Think of your loved ones at home . . .
but not with thoughts of sad regret, your friends with
love will clasp you yet. God, the almighty one will save
and guide the children of the brave.[7]

Far more elaborate ceremonies were staged in wealthy
communities. In the Black Belt town of Hayneville, plantation mistresses provided opulent entertainment lasting
several days for two recently organized companies. It
consisted of a series of gala events that included suppers,
dances, and inspirational speeches rendered by village
notables and by young girls dressed in "Alabama-made
homespun" as a mark of independence from Northern-
made textiles. The high point of the festivities consisted
of a mammoth banquet in which the "protectors of the
Southland" were served large amounts of barbecued
meats, fried chicken, vegetables of every sort, and large
bowls of boiled custard dotted with islands of whipped
cream. It was undoubtedly a well-fed and deeply inspired
group of men that marched out of town waving a bright
red banner bearing the inscription "Our Homes, Our
Rights, We Intrust to Your Keeping, Brave Sons of
Alabama."[8]

In neighboring Selma, the "Magnolia Cadets" received the same kind of treatment. This unit was almost
exclusively manned by the plantation gentry, but since they
served in the ranks it was looked upon as proof positive
that the Confederacy was not engaging in "a rich man's
war and a poor man's fight." However, the flag presentation ceremonies attracted widespread attention because
the donor, Elodia Todd, was a half-sister of Mrs. Abraham Lincoln and was engaged to the company's commander. After exhorting the men to great military glory

she presented "an elegant silken banner" for them to carry in combat against the United States.[9]

While those Army units composed of relatives and friends received the greatest amount of attention, there were some women who favored the Confederate Navy. In Mobile, ensigns were made for war vessels stationed in nearby waters and young girls were selected to preside over presentation ceremonies. During a period in 1863 when Huntsville was free of Northern occupation, a women's club commissioned a Richmond firm, at a cost of fourteen hundred dollars, to make the flag for the gunboat *Huntsville*. The finished product measured eighteen by twenty feet and contained the motto: "In God We Have Put Our Trust—Presented by the Ladies of Huntsville." This flag created a minor sensation when it was unfurled, and one Richmond editor wrote that it was the most elaborate and costly one in the entire nation.[10]

Patriotism drove scores of women to do more than make flags and speeches. As they saw it, their first task was to build an army and many became, in effect if not officially, the Confederacy's most successful recruiting officers during the early months of the war. Very few expected a long war and for this reason no great personal sacrifice was envisioned by those mothers who offered their sons to the services. Immediately after learning of Lincoln's call for 75,000 volunteers, Maria Ellington of Russell County went into the field where her two sons were working and demanded that the the duration of hostilities.[11] While War Meeting" at Florence, anothe excited by the plea for recruits th offered her dozen sons for servic "large enough to bear arms."[12] Ano *nom de plume* of "Nelle," wrote a letter to a Mont-gomery paper urging all mothers to surrender their sons. Furthermore, she advised, if those who enlisted fell in battle, make sure "your feet be to the foe, your back to the earth and your eyes gazing proudly . . . upon high heaven's . . . vaulted dome, entrusting yourselves in His care Who is the God of war."[13]

However, it was the younger women who exerted the greatest pressure on the men to join the army. "The un-married ladies were so patriotic," wrote a soldier from Selma, "that every able-bodied young man was constrained to enlist."[14] The early successes of Confederate arms caused scores of teen-age girls to become especially active in goading laggards and cowards into the services. It was not an easy job and at best a distasteful one, but many a reluctant patriot was cajoled, badgered, and oftentimes shamed into doing his duty. In nearly every community the press called for organized campaigns to promote enlist-ment drives. On November 30, 1861, a Selma editor, for example, suggested that all young women of the com-munity should adopt a policy of "pout and sulk" until their sweethearts volunteered.[15]

The challenge was eagerly accepted and Selma girls launched a crusade against those men not in the army. Looking upon male civilians as some kind of freak, one "pretty blue eyed rolliking lassie" announced publicly that she would refuse to date any man not in uniform.[16] An-other proclaimed that she would never marry a civilian in wartime and preferred to remain an old maid, if such became necessary, to win the war against "the hateful Yankees."[17] Moreover, she advised the females of Ala-bama to do likewise, for such tactics would solve the prob-lem of filling the Southern army. At least one Selma belle broke her engagement when her fiancé failed to enlist before the marriage date. She also sent him a skirt and female undergarments with the terse message: "Wear these or volunteer."[18] The women of Selma never relented in their drive and in 1863 a sizable group held a convention for the express purpose of "effectually securing the safety of every faint-hearted brother" not yet in service. They hit upon the plan of sending all laggards across the Northern lines and offered to pay transportation costs, provided such persons would register with a committee of the convention so that the names could be made public.[19]

Recruiting activities were put into practice in other Alabama communities, but there were areas where young women remained quite indifferent to the marital spirit. A Troy paper accused the ladies of that southeastern town of being "practical loafers" for not doing anything in behalf of encouraging enlistments. The editor considered such apathy dangerous and more responsible for destroying the young men's patriotism than "all causes put together."[20] Stung by this reproach, a "Patriotic Ladies Association" was formed for the purpose of getting men to volunteer.[21] By 1863 this group enlarged its scope and goals when its members agreed "to plant corn and raise meat for the army" and further pledged themselves to "pull up, cut up, and destroy . . . every acre of cotton" that was being cultivated in violation of the government's request for more food crops.[22] The Trojans thought it such a good idea that they recommended that all Southern women should follow their lead.

The passage of conscription measures tended to diminish the women's recruiting enterprises, but the press urged them to continue using their influence in getting men to re-enlist after the completion of military obligations. The

editor of a Grove Hill paper published several letters
from wives pleading with husbands to sign up for extra
terms of duty.[23] The aunt of a Wilcox County soldier advised her nephew *"not to come home"* even though he was
eligible for discharge. She pointed out that his honor was
at stake and went on to write that she refused to believe
that he was capable of forsaking his "country, now, nor
will I believe it until I hear it from your own lips."[24]

Women with relatives in the services bitterly assailed
draft-dodgers as cowards and traitors and took special
pains to criticize those women whose menfolks remained
at home. "Ruth of Uniontown," Alabama, became out-
raged on seeing "fine ruddy stout-looking gentlemen" not
in uniform on the streets of Selma. She had overheard one
of them answer an inquiry of why he was not in the army
with "his wife would not let him go." Such an excuse was
totally unacceptable to her and the irate patriot went on
record in assuring the wife in question, through a letter to
a local newspaper, that the majority of Alabama women
would be only too happy "to plant and sow, reap and mow,
while her lawful protector was on the battlefields shedding
blood to keep her in peace and quietness."[25]

Even when the war took unfavorable turns for the
Southern cause, a few continued supporting enlistment
activities. In 1864 Margaret Canedo of Mobile came out
with a song entitled "Re-enlistment." Described as a
"spontaneous song of the heart" the last of eight verses
called on every able-bodied male to:

> Plant the flag-staff in the earth,
> And round it rally, every son
> Who loves the State that gave him birth,
> What though our limbs be weak?

What though we bear full many a scar?
Huzza! here's to our native soil!
We'll enlist, and for the war![26]

While the martial spirit ran high, however, some of Alabama's most militant female patriots dreamed of a military career, but only a daring few attempted to translate such dreams into reality. The closest that any came to military service was in ill-fated attempts at organizing home-guard forces. In June of 1861, for example, a small group in Gainesville undertook to form such a unit composed of the community's women. The promoters argued that since most of the men were in the army, law and order were in danger of a breakdown, and besides: "It would not be amiss for us to accustom ourselves to the smell of gunpowder, the loading of guns, pistols, etc. . . ." in case of invasion.[27] Interested females were requested to assemble at a local hotel, enroll their names, and begin basic training. The project failed to materialize when too few volunteers appeared for duty, but those who did organized a soldiers' aid society. A year later, a Mobile woman, obviously itchy for a fight, wrote:

> If there are not men enough in Mobile, we are willing to go down to the batteries and work in the mud and sand as did our sisters at Leyden and Harlem; and when the hurtling hail rains down upon us, if the men quail, a Maid of Saragossa will be found behind every cannon . . . [28]

Fortunately, the need never arose for "a Maid of Saragossa" at Mobile's fortifications, and existing records do not reveal whether or not any Alabama woman ever fought in the army.

Personal encounters with Northern soldiers were rare occurrences at the beginning of the Civil War, but those who came face-to-face with Yankees seized the opportunity to dramatically demonstrate their patriotism with outbursts of defiance. Most of these events occurred outside the state, as did the incident that took place near Appalachicola, Florida, aboard a ship captured while attempting to run the Federal blockade. When the Union officer ordered the ship's flag lowered, a Mrs. F. Holland of Greenville, Alabama, sprang into action, seized the flag from the deck and "wrapped it around her and dared the officer to touch it. . . ." Absolutely refusing the pleas of her husband and other passengers to let go, she "protested that she would die" rather than surrender "the holy banner." There she stood, wrapped in the Confederate flag, as the amused officer ordered a one-gun salute in honor of the intrepid patriot from Alabama.[29]

Augusta J. Evans, an ever-faithful Confederate, expressed the wish "to touch off a *red hot ball*" at a Yankee-held fort near Norfolk, while on a visit to the Virginia city in 1861. She wrote the following detailed account of her two-day experiences under fire:

A few days since I went to Sewell's Point to visit some Georgia friends . . . and during my stay went to an exposed point to look at Fortress Monroe. . . . While I stood looking . . . the immense Rifle Cannon at the Rip-Raps thundered angrily, and to my amazement, a heavy shell exploded a few *yards* from us. I turned my glass at once on the Rip-Raps, and distinctly *saw* the muzzle of the villainous gun *pointed* at our party; saw the gunmen at work *reloading,* and while I watched a second flash sent its missile of death right *at us.* When a *third* ball whizzed over our heads . . . the officers *insisted* we should get out of sight. . . . How I long for a secession flag to shake *defiantly* in their teeth at every fire. . . . Ten shells fell on land, but 'Nobody was hurt.'[30]

Augusta returned the following day for another round of firing and later wrote to a friend that the two days in which she became a target constituted the most eventful time of her life.

Every war produces heroes for civilians to adore and cherish, but never has hero-worship reached such giddy heights as in the Civil War, when military eminence went hand-in-hand with moral fervor. To scores of romantic-minded women in Alabama, the war was a joust between good and bad knights in which Southern warriors who represented the "just cause" deserved victory and all the adoration that noncombatants could give them. The military hero became a breed apart from ordinary men. He was nearly always an officer in fancy dress uniform riding a prancing steed against the enemies of his country. Many a school girl's heart skipped a beat when the names of Lee, Jackson, and Beauregard came up in conversation, or when she read newspaper accounts of their battles. On the other hand, enlisted men were generally ignored, except possibly in the private esteem of their immediate families and close friends.

Prominent among the long list of martial heroes was General P. G. T. Beauregard of Louisiana. He seemed to be especially made for hyperbole; Creole French, dark and handsome, he became a living legend to a host of admiring females. Even his horse came in for a share of admiration, if for no other reason than the animal's close proximity to its rider. A Huntsville girl came into possession of some tail hair from the horse Beauregard had ridden at First Manassas and sent two strands to a friend in Selma as a treasured keepsake.[31] However, his most ardent admirer was Augusta J. Evans, who kept up a lively correspondence with the general throughout the war and for many years after its close. She often wrote to him of her wartime activities, but more frequently she expressed the highest kind of praise for his military abilities.

While spending the summer of 1862 in Mobile, Beauregard came into close contact with the Alabama authoress. In fact, he found such pleasure in her company that he guiltily confessed to a friend: "It would not do for me to see her too often, for I might forget 'home and country' in their hour of need and distress."[32] Miss Evans was not alone in having a crush on Beauregard nor did he ever seem anxious to discourage female admiration. He found Mobile "a city of beauties" and after leaving for duty corresponded with several fans there. One of them sent him a note in which his sons were called the "busy B's" and their father "the king B of the hive." In replying, the general obviously spoke as the "king B" when he wrote: "Rest assured that he will never forget *where* the prettiest & sweetest flowers are to be found for the honey of his hive."[33]

Women from all walks of life indulged in hero-worship, but few had the personal pleasure of meeting their heroes in person as Kate Cumming did during the years she worked with the perambulating hospitals attached to the Army of Tennessee. General Sterling Price first attracted her attention because he was "one of the finest looking men on horseback" she had ever seen and he bore a very remarkable resemblance to the much-admired Lord Ragland of the British army. This spinster's admiration, however, was based on more solid grounds—his willingness to share

the hardships of camp life and the dangers of the battlefields with his men—rather than on personal appearance
alone. But in the case of General John H. Morgan no
excuse for veneration was necessary. His eyes alone won
Kate's unrequited admiration because they reminded her
of "a description of Burns by Walter Scott" and they
"fairly glowed with animation" as he enthralled her with
accounts of his military experiences. When Morgan left
for the battlefronts she and a colleague unashamedly admitted that they would rather see him "than any of our
great men."[34] Not all military leaders won Kate's respect.
In 1863 she condemned Braxton Bragg for military reverses. She was, nevertheless, kinder in her estimate of
Joseph E. Johnston's failures, mainly because he had
acted "as well as he can with his means." And, after the
fall of Atlanta, she took comfort in the rationalization
that Southern forces under Hood did not "loose nearly as
many [men] as the enemy."[35]

For every Confederate hero there was more than
double the number of Yankee villains for Alabama women
to scorn and even hate bitterly. They raised a storming
fury, the likes of which was unexpected from the legendary ladies of the old South. Yet they offered neither excuse nor explanation for the many one-woman assaults on
the enemies of their beloved Southern republic. Their
cause was too noble and patriotic for temperate language
or thoughts, and many went far beyond the area of responsible expression. From the beginning Lincoln became the
prime target of ridicule; he was depicted as the arch-
enemy of Southerners, and a bungling politician to be held
solely responsible for bringing on the war.

To some superpatriots he was nothing more than an
abolitionist fanatic dedicated to the amalgamation of the

races. On the day following the firing on Fort Sumter, Sarah Lowe, a student at Huntsville Female College, saw the war as the South's best opportunity to show Lincoln "that we are not his negresses."[36] All ages seemed to take sublime pleasure in heaping abuse upon the president of the United States. Even elementary school girls expressed strong dislike for Lincoln, and a few wrote him insulting letters containing their thoughts. A ten-year-old pupil at Chapel Academy in Uchee wrote the president, under the name of "Little Secessionist," that he "need not be boasting about driving the South back into the Union, no indeed! for our brave Southern people . . . will never be ruled by old Abe Lincoln nor darkey [Hannibal] Hamlin either. . . ."[37]

Everything poured forth from the pens of these purveyors of Lincoln hate. From their testimony he emerged as one of the great monsters of the nineteenth century. Gossip about him was served up with malice and demeaning remarks made to emphasize his inhuman character. A surprising number believed him capable of the worst kind of iniquities. Kate Cumming recorded in her memoirs many entries castigating Lincoln without restraint or without checking the sources of the rumors she heard while working in Confederate hospitals. On one occasion in 1863 she accused him of personally refusing to exchange prisoners-of-war. It was, to her, "the cruelest act of which he was guilty, not only to us, but to his own men." Since the Confederate government was unable adequately to feed and care for its own men, then "how can he expect us to feed his?" Lincoln was a heartless man to Kate even in his actions toward Northerners and she mused sadly that:

Human lives are nothing to him; all the prisoners we

have might die of starvation, and I do not expect they
would cost him a thought, as all he has to do is issue
a call for so many thousands to be offered up on his
altars of sacrifice.[38]

Other prominent United States officials came in for
serious condemnation. When Andrew Johnson was inaugurated as vice president in 1864, Mrs. W. D. Chadick
of Huntsville made some catty remarks in her diary about
the affair, an account of which she had read in a Kentucky
newspaper. From this source she was willing to believe
that the vice president was "gloriously drunk" because he
proclaimed himself and Lincoln to be of plebeian origin.
It was to her not only an ungraceful remark, but a hypocritical one in light of Mrs. Lincoln's expensive dress of
"black silk velvet . . . trimmed in ermine" which rendered
"the whole scene from beginning to end . . . quite a
farce."[39] Lincoln's second election was viewed by Martha
Foster Crawford, an Alabama Baptist missionary in
China, with deep forebodings for the Confederacy. It
was proof enough to her that the Northern people intended "to continue the war to the last extreme . . . to
go on to the entire extermination of the South."[40]

As the war progressed, the list of villains was enlarged
to include all Northerners, regardless of sex or position.
Many became convinced that their prewar leaders were
correct in branding every Yankee as an abolitionist fanatic.
In 1862 Minerva Abercrombie felt this way when she was
told that a letter written by a Northern girl, which had
been found on a dead soldier, contained abolition senti-
ments, along with the request not to return home until "he
had killed *Six Rebels*." Now she was more than ever
convinced that Yankees were brainwashed from infancy
with

the seeds of abolitionism and cultivated with such care
and so identified with their very existence that any attempt to eradicate them would be like separating the
soul from the body.[41]

And such was the fate that she prescribed for all enemy
soldiers and civilians.

Some broke relations with Southern friends who had
sided with the United States. Augusta J. Evans did not
mince words when she wrote Mary V. Terhune about how
mortifying it was to know that a friend and "a Southern
woman should disgrace her section" by remaining "at the
North living contentedly among the oppressors of the
only free people left upon the American continent." Nor
did the Mobile authoress want any part of friendship
from Almira Hart Phelps, the headmistress of the
Patapsco Female Institute near Baltimore, Maryland. As
a teacher and textbook writer, the Phelps woman came
under double suspicion; she might contaminate young
minds with Northern ideas and, what was worse, she
"sympathized with the unscrupulous wretches who are
invading Southern soil. . . ."[42]

Invasion of the South deepened the noncombatants'
animosity and supplied additional objects for hatred.
Northern commanders were singled out for special abuse
because it was believed that they took pride in conducting
war against defenseless civilians. According to Kate Cumming, Sherman's campaign in Georgia was

almost equal to anything of which the Sepoys were
guilty. Negro regiments, officered by men with white
skins, but with black hearts as black as night, have been
turned loose on the helpless inhabitants and encouraged
to do their worst.[43]

When Florence, Alabama, surrendered in 1862, a young woman of Huntsville used such invectives as "vandals," "barbarians," "Yankee hirelings," "Northern marauders," and "shameless outlaws," in a single letter to describe her feelings about the victorious army.[44] The fall of New Orleans caused one woman to wish for "the strong arm of 'Yellow Jack'" in dealing with the "arch fiend Picayune Butler" and his army of occupation.[45]

Even those bearing devoutly religious reputations used strong language, such as Martha Jane Crossley of Perote, who recorded how her "blood chills" over Northern "attrocities" and asked in her prayers that "God will not always suffer such wrongs" to continue indefinitely.[46] A few advocated the adoption of a scorched-earth policy in hurting the Northern forces, if such should become necessary. On several occasions Kate Cumming expressed the wish that Mobile be burned rather than allow it to come under "the foot of the vandal foe." By 1865 Kate had a change of mind and recommended that her home town be surrendered in order "to save towns of the interior, which will be of more use to us" in ultimately winning the war.[47]

The loyalty and patriotism of Alabama's Confederate women did not pass unnoticed. From time to time the press contained laudatory editorials on their role in the war, and the General Assembly was very generous in expressing gratitude in the form of resolutions. In 1864, for example, the law-makers "being profoundly and gratefully impressed with the lofty and patriotic spirit, and the ardent devotion . . . of the noble women of the State . . . hereby tender[s] to them our thanks, and the thanks of the whole people of the State."[48]

3

Hurrah for the ladies! they are the soul of the war. . . .

From the very beginning of the war a great many Alabama women recognized the need for keeping the morale of the fighting forces at the highest possible level. Upon the Confederate army were centered their hopes for survival as a nation and along with it the perpetuation of the Southern way of life for their posterity. Very few of them, if any, required any coaxing from government agencies, the church, or the press in performing this most familiar and personal service. It had always been one of woman's specialties to supply encouragement for her menfolk and she fell into the role of comforter with even more zeal during the trying times of war. Keeping fighting men happy was not a superficial thing, but something calling for imagination, hard work, and inconvenience. Yet it was not always an unpleasant chore, for many a young woman enjoyed herself immensely while cheering the men in gray.

The vast majority of morale-boosters were not political philosophers by profession; they had never been trained beyond the usual schooling for females of the day; their field was that of homemaker and for the most part they were either married to or engaged to a soldier. All of them had male relatives or friends in the services who at one time or another needed some form of encouragement from the home front. In supplying this need they made use of every device within their power to vivify the spirits of the men as well as their own. During the early months, women gathered at depots and along the line of march to dispense cheerfulness and refreshments among soldiers on the way to training camps or battlefields. Some went aboard congested troop trains and mingled with the men while others called out encouraging words from the sidelines.

When the Fourth Alabama Regiment paused for a short time in Tuskegee, a delegation of young girls literally showered one "little captain . . . with bouquets of flowers," after which box lunches were given out until the supplies were exhausted.[1] Others went to great trouble in providing little comforts that gladden the hearts of soldiers away from home for the first time. Some, like Anna M. Washburn of Montgomery, took a wagon load of "delecacies as well as the substantials of life" to an Alabama unit quartered near Pensacola and personally supervised the distribution of her gifts.[2]

It was not uncommon for women to prepare large amounts of food and drink on short notice for troops passing through their communities. In 1862, James B. Hall of Autauga County told of having a "glorious time" while enroute from Montgomery to Chattanooga. He wrote that women at every station in Alabama "met us with fruits and all kinds of eatables," and in one place volunteer workers suddenly appeared with "cart loads of meat, bread, cabbage, etc." Hall accorded the highest kind of praise for Alabama's morale-builders and credited them with doing more to raise his flagging spirits than any others he had encountered since leaving home. In his estimation they were far more humane than Mississippi women, whom he found so heartless that they would rather "a soldier perish for water before you could ever see a lady bringing water for them."[3]

As the war quickened in pace, depot demonstrations became a hindrance to the swift movement of troops and in some cases military authorities prohibited them. This action brought howls of protest from those who had already planned leave-taking affairs for local service men. An Opelika group, for instance, considered one such order "a shameful and detestable outrage" and submitted a petition for publication in a local newspaper severely scolding authorities for depriving them "of the privilege of pressing the hands of our Brothers, Sons, Husbands, and Friends" on their way to an uncertain future. They also expressed keen disappointment in not being able to present the gifts of food and flowers that they had gone to so much trouble to prepare.[4]

There were no official objections raised against the great variety of other privately sponsored projects to cheer thousands of soldiers stationed in Alabama. Both amateur and experienced hostesses took a hand in organizing some form of entertainment for the pleasure of officers and men in the ranks. One of the most persistent and popular diversions were *Tableaux Vivants,* with casts of fresh young school girls and generally depicting a patriotic theme. On Christmas Eve of 1861, the faculty and students of Cedar Hill Academy near Demopolis staged one such production, which they boasted would rival anything produced by the French Opera at New Orleans. The high point of the evening's festivities came with the tableaux representing the Confederacy. It consisted of a still scene in which eleven young students, each bearing the label of one of the Confederate States, were arranged in pyramidal form. At the summit stood a girl bearing the name "Alabama," vigorously waving the Confederate flag as the band played "Dixie." Clustered around the base were those representing Southern states still in the Union. One, for example, was on her knees as "Weeping Kentucky," gazing imploringly at the "stars and bars." Another, designated "Maryland," was dressed in mourning cloth, beseeching a Confederate officer who stood nearby to protect her from a sword that a Federal soldier was holding menacingly over her.[5] And so on, in a melodramatic way, were depicted the other nonConfederate border states. Similar themes were produced throughout the state during the war years and became favorites among Alabama audiences.

A big hit with the soldiers were dances, given mainly by those women whose religious faith permitted this form of amusement. However, dancing parties, or balls, which name identified the more formal affairs, proliferated to such an extent that one suspects that many girls compromised their religious scruples in behalf of the "great" cause of raising the soldiers' morale. While older women acted as chaperones, younger ones furnished merriment and partnership for service men of all ages who were eager to forget army life in the arms of a pretty girl. The most splendid affairs were nearly always officers' balls, and young ladies usually preferred these, because of better opportunities of making a proper liaison, to enlisted men's dances.

Not all scorned the men in the ranks, according to James B. Hall, who wrote of being "perfectly carried away . . . by the young ladies of Florence" in 1864. At a dance of mixed officers and enlisted men he enjoyed the supreme pleasure of giving a "pretty rough push" to a high-ranking officer who had accidentally stepped on his partner's dress. Florence girls won this private's unqualified admiration and he gave one credit for momentarily diverting his mind from the deadly business of war. "Last night I was chatting with a gay young lady," he mused happily, but on second thought, reflected, "tomorrow night I may be far away on the march."[6]

The women of Florence had good reasons for being nice to Confederate soldiers. Their city was invaded several times during the war and they exerted special efforts to keep morale high among their Confederate protectors when they were in control. The owners of large mansions furnished elegant settings for many social affairs, which catered principally to officers stationed in and near the beleagured city. In 1864, while in Florence, Lieutenant Aristide Hopkins of New Orleans registered amazement on discovering in the north Alabama city a polite and cultured society that in many ways rivaled his home city's. He made the comparison after visiting "a splendid house, with a sumptuously furnished parlor," in which he was welcomed by "six unusually pretty young ladies" who conversed with him in "a polite and polished manner," something he had long despaired of finding outside his beloved New Orleans. Of special interest was "Miss C," whom the snobbish officer found "as remarkable for her beauty as for her wit," and he made every effort to spend much time in her company. In general, Hopkins found all Alabama women "more patriotic, prettier, and used less snuff than in certain portions of N. Ga."[7]

Huntsville women were also moved with a lively desire to raise the morale of Confederate service men but, as elsewhere, they too showed a preference for entertaining officers. In 1862, before the Northern invasion, General William Hardee and his staff were frequent visitors at evening socials held in the elegant homes of the rich. The general, a widower, won the reputation of being "particularly devoted to the ladies," and they seemed to return the compliment, for he was often seen driving about town "in a calash & mules *full of ladies*."[8] The same situation prevailed at Mobile, where officers attended the best parties, went to the better balls, and escorted the daughters of prominent families to musicales and theaters. Such was the experience of George W. Gift, a young naval officer from Georgia assigned to duty aboard the *C.S.S. Gaines* on Mobile Bay. Although he was an engaged man, he nevertheless partook of the glittering social life of the invasion-free city, but always gave full accounts of the activities to his fiancée. He told her of attending teas and balls, and on one occasion was pleased to inform her that he had been a guest in the homes of such local luminaries as Augusta J. Evans and Octavia Levert.[9]

On the other hand, scores of Alabama women became especially active in providing warm welcomes for local soldiers on leave, regardless of rank. Nothing seemed too good for the native veterans, and their return invariably inaugurated a round of parties, dances, and banquets prepared with loving care by women of remote villages and towns. When a fortunate few of the Perote Guards came home on furlough in 1862, they were treated "as conquering heroes." Social affairs were daily occurrences and provided the setting for many reunions of sweethearts and friends; a soldier named Edward McMorries waxed romantic as he wrote of the personal experience of "soft eyes looked, love to eyes, that spoke again" at one such gathering. He may have been a "conquering hero" to the village girls, but his condition changed drastically in urban areas. While on the outskirts of Mobile, McMorries discovered to his sorrow that "Southern women . . . could not resist . . . a Confederate soldier with brass bars and stars on his coat collar." He went on to register the familiar lament that only a few found "some fascination in a corporal's stripes."[10]

Despite the corporal's accurate estimate of the facts of life, there were some men who found many Alabama girls more than willing to keep company with ordinary soldiers. This was especially true of those stationed in the central and southern parts of the state, which escaped invasion until the last year of the war. Here enterprising young swains on furlough discovered a happy hunting ground for female companionship. Instead of resenting the advantages officers enjoyed over enlisted men, Private Sam Watkins of the First Tennessee Regiment allied with a young lieutenant and literally used him as bait in attracting a girl for himself. According to Watkins, they succeeded in meeting "a couple of beautiful and interesting young ladies" from Selma and frolicked with them until "the wee sma' hours" of the morning.[11] Others, like William A. Sivley of North Carolina, played the field and kept a romance going with two sweethearts at the same time while he was stationed near Montevallo in 1864. As if completely oblivious of his own infidelity, he once wrote to a friend that while on a date with his Montevallo girl, he was suddenly smitten with the desire to see his "other sweetheart" who lived out of town. It was his opinion that the country girl was fonder of him and besides, she was "as pretty as red shoes with blue strings in them."[12]

Understandably, many young girls became positively fascinated with the handsome young strangers in their community and more than a few made considerable efforts to become a soldier's sweetheart. Attaching no importance to the fact that Henry Clay Reynolds was married, three "fine looking Mountain girls" living near Gadsden claimed him as their own and categorically refused to believe that he had a wife in North Carolina. When one of them watched Reynolds lead a charge against "thirty Blue Bellies" in a field adjacent to her house, she was so impressed that she ran to her mother and wailed inconsolably that the dashing soldier "belonged to Her, wife or no wife." In writing to his spouse of the episode, Reynolds teasingly ended his letter with: *"Now Sweet, don't get jealous."*[13]

When the northern part of the state came under Union occupation in 1862, the majority of the region's women treated their captors with the utmost scorn and at first refused any social intercourse with the enemy. Yet, there were rare occasions in which a few responded amicably to the entreaties of lonesome Yankees anxious for female company. At least one, James W. Riley of an Illinois regiment, persuaded one rebel of Decatur to become his sweetheart. The affair lasted for over two months and from time to time he even had her arrange dates for his comrades in arms. On one of these occasions, Riley and a fellow soldier had to slip across Confederate lines at dusk to meet their dates in a rural cabin, and when the foursome began to enjoy themselves, or, as Riley tells it: "Just as we thought everything was lovely, and the Goose Hung High, here comes the Johnnies, charging down on the house." The Yankee lovers were forced into a hasty retreat, but suspecting that a trap had been set, Riley returned the following day for an explanation. When he was told that it was the noise that had attracted the Confederates, he was satisfied and continued dating the girl until his unit moved on.[14]

More than a few others made similar liaisons, but in 1864 there were at least two unidentified Yankees who came to a tragic end over the affections of a capricious country girl living near Huntsville. When the two in question discovered that they were in love with the same girl, they agreed to fight a duel—the winner getting all. Army rifles were chosen as weapons and both parties fired at the same time and both were killed on the spot. In reporting the incident, Lucius W. Barber made the wry comment to his fellow soldiers that they should not "have more than one sweetheart at a time."[15]

The persistent rejection of the men of the occupation forces drove a few into social intercourse with Negro women. In this respect, little or no official sanctions were imposed against those who made discreet liaisons; nor were there any hard and fast rules regarding attending racially mixed social affairs. According to Lloyd Jenkins Jones, when a ball was announced for the evening of January 16, 1864, the men of his unit flocked to the ball and when they found that it was "a nigger dance," some left, but "others enjoyed the joke by 'tripping with the colored' sisters." Ordinary Yankee soldiers suffered the same fate as their counterparts in the Confederate army. United States officers enjoyed every advantage with women, yet Jones recorded with glee how an enlisted men's ball attended by forty local girls excelled "the shoulder straps fizzle" of an earlier date.[16]

Not all contacts with enemy soldiers were of a romantic nature. Alabama women, as was true of Southerners elsewhere, nursed wounded Yankees and performed other small acts of kindness, although passionately devoted to their cause and country. On rare occasions a few went to great lengths in helping to relieve the suffering of the Yankee prisoners-of-war located in Alabama. The intolerable conditions prevailing at Castle Morgan near Cahaba so distressed Amanda Gardner that she went out of her way to help. She hit upon the idea of deputizing her pre-teenage daughter to smuggle food and clothing in to the men. During the winter months she donated carpets for use as blankets and occasionally included books along with boxes of foodstuffs.

All of this activity was permitted by sympathetic guards, but once when an unfriendly sentinel caught the Gardner girl passing supplies, she and her mother were arrested and brought before the prison's commander. Both were released after receiving a stern warning never to come into contact with the prisoners in the future. Although Amanda professed strong Confederate sympathies, she blithely ignored the warning and continued her charities. For her services one inmate later wrote of her as "a human angel," whose memory deserved to be "cherished with feelings of reverence by the men who were grateful witnesses of her angelic deeds. . . ."[17]

Like men in all wars, Alabamians suffered from homesickness and spent many waking hours thinking of their womenfolk back home. Some longed to be with relatives, but most of those stationed in battle areas far from Alabama concentrated their thoughts on future reunions with wives and sweethearts. The constant company of nothing but men day in and day out, sometimes stretching on for months, took a terrible toll on the soldiers' morale. The absence of feminine companionship was a greater cause of despondency than any other, and army life became an intolerable existence. But many a young male refused to be lonely and took his pleasures in the company of a woman whenever and wherever he could find it. Before arriving at Winchester, Virginia, in 1861, Frank Harralson of Selma had given up seeing women until after the war, but upon meeting a local girl he immediately fell in love and wrote his aunt that she should not be "surprised if you didn't have a little niece soon."[18] Robert Tutwiler once told his sisters of finding Virginia "a truly interesting place," mainly because it was filled with *"such* beauties I can play with . . ." that he thought he should be excused for being "inconstant toward the Ala. girls. . . ."[19]

Having equally as good reasons for admiring Virginia morale-boosters was Hillary A. Herbert of Butler County, Alabama. According to his own account, he moved in the highest social circles, dated and cavorted with several of the Old Dominion's lighthearted women during the times he was free of military duty. Willing to try anything for fun, he once volunteered to play the role of knight in a "medieval" tournament sponsored by a women's club of Orange Court House. All the trappings of a Scott novel were present: gaily colored pennants, sabers, and shields decorated with mock coats-of-arms. The climax of the festivities called for a tilting contest "at rings with swords," with the highest scorer awarded the prize of crowning his "lady the Queen of Love and Beauty." Unfortunately, the premier performance was canceled when the cast was called to perform in the less dramatic duty of fighting real Yankee soldiers.[20]

Rarely did ordinary soldiers have the opportunity for courting girls in the soldier-crowded Richmond areas, for here, too, officers received preferential treatment as companions. Men without rank were not always neglected, however, and capital-city women were often seen handing

out gifts of food and tobacco to those Alabama units passing through on the way to the front. "We found the ladies
still kind here," wrote Crenshaw Hall in 1864; "several
hats and loaves of bread were given some of the bareheads
and one old lady gave a barefooted man a nice pair of
English shoes and a pair of socks."[21]

Circumstances changed somewhat for those regiments
located in less populous sections and many sought satisfactory social outlets by visits in the countryside. Frequently,
but not always, entire regiments became the recipients of
a gratifying amount of attention from Virginia's country
girls. From testimony given by Colonel William C. Oates,
the commander of the Fifteenth Alabama, it would seem
that his men had discovered an Islamic-kind of paradise
in the Blue Ridge country. They not only found "Virginia's
peasantry intensely Southern in sentiment," but extremely
well disposed in welcoming every man into their homes.
Many young bachelors found sweethearts and some married men became "half inclined to turning Mormon and
marrying again, at least for during the war." Oates himself could not agree more with this point of view, for he
too found the girls "so pretty and friendly" that it was
understandable how so many had succumbed to "the weak-
ness of amiability."[22]

Although it is extremely doubtful if other regiments enjoyed the same grand time, there were nevertheless many
incidents of kindness showed Alabamians by women in
other states of the Confederacy. While on the march in
Tennessee, for example, Robert Bliss told of seeing elderly
matrons giving pails of water to thirsty soldiers and
younger ones wishing them well with words and affection-
ate gestures. At one place he saw a very old woman drawing water from her well and he calculated that she had

been at this work from "dawn to dusk." Speaking for his regiment he was sure that that old woman received "many a soldier's blessing" for her thoughtfulness.[23]

Men in general, and particularly soldiers, rarely leave detailed records of amorous dalliance with prostitutes. Such matters usually are conversation topics in the barracks for impressing timid comrades, or remain locked forever in the memory of wartime experiences. Doubtlessly many more than the records show shed their nineteenth-century inhibitions and, out of sheer biological necessity, raised their morale with prostitutes. Nearly every Southern city had its tenderloin district, but Richmond outstripped all others and became a mecca for the world's oldest profession. But prostitution also flourished in rural areas and especially in those places where large concentrations of soldiers offered the best opportunities for prospective customers. In 1864, Private Orville C. Bumpass wrote home from north Alabama that "the state of morals is quite as low as the soil, almost all the women are given to whoredom & the ugliest, shallowfaced, shaggy headed, bare footed dirty wretches you ever saw."[24]

The year before, Major W. J. Mims wrote his wife from a camp in eastern Tennessee that "prostitutes are thickly crowded through mountain & valley, in hamlet & city," but none were able to "woo me successfully for a moment from the path of duty to the treacherous embrace." Mims went on partially to blame the presence of large numbers of soldiers for the existing conditions, since many of them "do not seem to feel the same restraints away from home, which at home regulated their intercourse with the gentler sex. . . ." Up to this point his premise may deserve some credibility, but he continued with the strange notion that "the poorer classes here were never as virtuous as in our southern latitudes where slavery abounds to a great extent. . . ."[25]

Homefront women also experienced feelings of lonesomeness and craved masculine companionship after their menfolk marched off to war. While most remained at home, nursing their sorrows and waiting for furlough time, a surprising number endured the countless hardships of wartime travel to be with their men in army camps and battlefields. More often than not affection was the main reason for army wives making such trips, but others were undoubtedly motivated by a desire to have a good time or to escape the boredom of a manless society at home. Others, married or unmarried, simply wanted excitement and there were those who just dropped in for a casual visit with army friends when they happened to be in the neighborhood. Regardless of the circumstances, female visitors always seemed to have an invigorating effect upon the men and went a long way in raising their morale to soaring heights.

At the beginning, some married women undertook to accompany their husbands to battle stations. For example, in 1861 Mollie Mitchell followed her husband's company from its point of departure at Shelby Springs, Alabama, to Iuka Springs, Mississippi. Yet, for all her trouble, Mollie was ordered home after only a short and uncomfortable reunion held in a local hotel.[26] The most persistent visitor was Mrs. W. D. Chadick. As a resident of Union-occupied Huntsville, she frequently arranged meetings with her husband while he was based in Confederate-controlled territory south of the Tennessee River. In one episode, she told of enduring the hazard of first eluding Federal pickets and then having to cross the river in a small and leaky boat. Upon meeting Colonel Chadick she thought the worst inconveniences were behind her, but before the two settled down in a prearranged trysting place they were forced to ride many miles while seated upon the same horse. Such an experience had little effect upon this woman's ardor for connubial reunions and she made many trips into what she called "Dixie" during the course of the war.

In some cases understanding commanders encouraged reunions in the field for the men under their command. Especially permissive in this matter was George W. Gift, while he served as executive officer aboard the river gunboat *Chattahoochie*. In 1863 he wrote his fiancée the following account of a conjugal visit of one of his sailors:

Last evening I gave him permission to remain on shore, as his wife had come to visit the bold Sailor. At the time I did not particularly notice the individual, but when I came upon his this morning I beheld the most rediculous sight that I have witnessed, probably in my whole life. The individual in question did not look like a man. He wore the uniform of the ship, though *very much soiled*. Over the . . . shirt he had drawn a brown close fitting coat which caused his arms to stand off from the body somewhat like wings, his general appearance was decidedly dingy. He was encamped under a live oak tree with his wife. She had a very strong resemblance to her 'worser' half, as regarded cleanliness. She wore no hoops and upon the whole she was the most woe begone outrageous batch of *oddities* I ever saw. She and the Conscript were partaking their morning meal. They were seated on the ground near each other and as I approached from behind, in no good humor, Conscript leaned towards his spouse and in a languid manner said *'Sugar give me a tater.'* She replied, 'Honey, I aint got Narry Neither.' My ire was forthwith appeased and retiring behind a neighboring tree I laughed immodestly.

The scene reminded me of two buzzards playing pigeons.[27]

Young and especially pretty visitors were always welcome sights and would set the entire camp gawking, even though officers had monopolized their company. The usual agenda included a tour of the camp and dinner at the officers' mess, followed by the exchange of light gossip and conversation about happenings back home. This procedure was followed by Colonel Thomas Hill Watts when a friend of his daughter, Lula Boykin, paid him a courtesy call in 1862 at a camp near Pensacola. As an added treat, the colonel decided to dress Miss Boykin as an officer to avoid detection as he took her on an evening inspection tour of the camp. At sentinel posts she was introduced as "Lieutenant Boykin," and while the two were enjoying discussing the ruse, Watts' horse got caught in quicksand and threw him to the ground. Fortunately, a squad of soldiers saw the accident and rushed to the rescue, and discovered that the lieutenant was a female. Alabama's future governor and his companion rode off with wet feet and a good deal of embarrassment. Shortly afterwards, Watts dutifully related the entire affair in a long letter to his daughter.[28]

As was to be expected, some enlisted men resented the privileges of the officers regarding women. William Hall was among those who thought "a camp is no place for wives," because "husbands cannot do two things at once, either wives or duty at camps must be neglected."[29] Indeed, quite a few husbands advanced every argument to dissuade their spouses from visiting them, but in many cases such advice went unheeded. Hugh Lawson Clay even enlisted the help of his sister-in-law in an effort to prevent his wife from joining him at Knoxville. It was pointed out that there were "insurmountable difficulties in the way of her coming," not the least of which was the high cost of living in Knoxville, where room rent alone amounted to a staggering four dollars a day for single accommodations.[30]

Although Clay succeeded in this instance, he failed to keep his wife away while he was stationed in other areas of the Confederacy. The Clay women were notoriously hard-headed and Virginia once had the idea of joining her husband after he was sent on a diplomatic mission to Canada in 1864. She pressured every official of her acquaintance and even asked President Davis to intercede in her behalf. Finally, she obtained the necessary passport and made arrangements with the Secretary of the Navy for passage on a blockade runner destined for Canada.[31] However, Clay scotched the venture with a firm negative, but only after promising to let her know of his welfare through coded messages that he would have published in Richmond newspapers.[32]

Not all women showed the same enthusiasm in cheering the men in gray and a few went out of their way to avoid any contact whatsoever with soldiers. This was especially true in urban centers where large concentrations of military personnel came into easy association with civilians at one time or another. The throngs of soldiers caused timid females to remain indoors for long periods of time, but when they did venture out, the prospect of being approached by strange men threw some into paroxysms of indignation and fear. When the New Orleans Zouaves came to Montgomery in 1861, their reputation for rowdy behavior had preceded them and concerned citizens took elaborate precautions for protecting their families from possible insult and injury. Heads of households ordered wives and children and even servants to remain at home until the dreaded Zouaves had left the city. Only Eliza Moore refused to believe the wild stories going around about these men. To her they were Confederate soldiers willingly risking their lives for the South and she determined to treat them hospitably even though "the command was not made up of the elite of Louisiana."[33] The opportunity came one hot July day as the Zouaves stood at ease in front of her residence after several hours of hard drilling. Mrs. Moore ordered her servants to serve water laced with molasses, to slake their thirst and to remind them of Louisiana's staple crop.

With the exception of invaded areas, Mobile women came into closer association with service men than any in the state. Here hundreds of bored and lonesome soldiers walked the streets in search of diversion, and the bolder ones acted as soldiers are expected to act, attempting to make liaisons with young women they chanced to meet. On witnessing such a contact in 1861, one citizen became so shocked that he called for official action to prevent a recurrence of insults "to modest and unoffending females of the city." According to his version, a group of Mississippi soldiers had made improper advances toward two ladies on St. Michael Street, and when they fled for sanctuary into a nearby church, the men followed them there, but fortunately the frightened women made an escape through a rear exit.[34] An immediate denial was registered with the local press in which the defendant, signing himself as "A Mississippi Volunteer," vigorously repudiated the charges. He took special pride in pointing out that it was impossible for Mississippians to become involved in untoward behavior because they were "good soldiers and gentlemen as well." And he went on to air a few grievances of his own regarding Mobile women. They were accused of treating his comrades "with frigid coldness" since their arrival and once more they had not bestirred themselves to give soldiers a drink of water during the hottest days of summer.[35] With this blast the matter rested, at least for a while.

As time went on, even more vigorous complaints were raised against the alleged high-handed attitudes of Mobile women. The denials were fewer and there was strong suspicion that all was not sweet accord between the soldiers and the women of the port city. For example, in 1862 "Junior" wrote a strong letter to a local editor protesting the shabby treatment accorded soldiers. What infuriated him most was overhearing one woman say that she "could not think of riding the city cars, because they were full of *common* soldiers!" Such a remark gave him special license to remind *"the common women of the city"* that the men whom she thought so beneath her were not in Mobile "by choice, but there to defend the Confederacy." He continued with a warning that if the "male and female, old and young, did not speedily correct this state of things and treat common soldiers with respect," he knew personally "many who would not raise a finger to keep the enemy from the city."[36]

Doubtless both sides in this rancorous controversy were ready to supply convincing reasons for their actions, but they were far from representing the typical point of view of soldiers on their relations with the women of Alabama. Indeed, great numbers of service men stationed in and beyond Alabama's borders had good reasons for counting blessings simply because women cared about their welfare and, in their own way, brought some cheer into each others' lives. At least one soldier thought that the distaff side of humanity deserved recognition, and he said so in a way that made him an unwitting spokesman for the mass of inarticulate service men. When Robert Bliss wrote an Alabama relative in 1863, he literally cried out in thanksgiving:

> Hurrah for the ladies! they are the soul of the war— had it not been for them the 'Rebellion' would have been crushed long ago, but as it is, by their energy and self-sacrificing devotion . . . they are cheering the men in the field.[37]

4

> . . . women's sphere of influence might be like Pascal's, "one of which the centre is everywhere, the circumference nowhere."

In 1863, after two years of pondering, Augusta Jane Evans reached the conclusion that little official responsibility had been assigned to women in the building of the Southern Confederacy. She was chagrined and frustrated about such waste of talent and unburdened her feelings in a long letter to General Beauregard. The loquacious authoress readily admitted it was inconceivable for females to don uniforms and to rush into battle, but they had much to offer to the struggling new nation without endangering man's monopoly of managing affairs of state. It was her contention that "women's sphere of influence might be like Pascal's, 'one of which the centre is everywhere, the circumference nowhere. . . .' "[1] The general had good reasons for appreciating this bit of feminine mystique from his Mobile friend, for she had already taken it upon herself to give him the benefit of her counsel on public issues and she stood ready to defend his military abilities against any kind of criticism.

Scores of Alabama women could not have agreed more with Miss Evans, even though many were personally familiar with either her views on the subject or her refer-

ence to Pascal's epigram. Like those of both sides of the
conflict, they required no prodding from anyone to offer
their services as confidantes and advisers, and even to engage as critics of the active participants of the war. Alabama women, as were Southerners everywhere, were privy
to every conceivable problem facing the Civil War generation, but none mounted rostrums, as did some few
Northern women, to express opinions on matters of public
interest. They still preferred the antebellum custom of
remaining in the background and they continued to confine
their views to letters, diaries, and conversations at tea
tables.

Despite this predilection, women from all walks of life
were called upon for assistance in assuring and corrobo-
rating the thoughts and actions of the men in their lives.
This was especially true of young men liable for military
duty at the beginning of the war. The day following
Alabama's secession, Alonzo B. Cohen of Carrollton
wrote his sister that he had recently joined a local company and was apprehensive about his future. In an unmis-
takable hint of fear he told of hearing cannon roaring all
week and that "the times are very hard and nothing is
talked of but war. . . ."[2] Shortly afterwards, Cohen again
wrote home and after acknowledging his sister's pep
talk went on to say that he and his comrades-in-arms were
now "only waiting for 'Old Abe' to come down with his
cohorts of abolitionists and we will . . . wipe them completely up."[3]

Such bursts of bravado were commonplace, but there
were also those in high places who did not hesitate to
inform home-front women of the true nature of the conflict. Major Hugh Lawson Clay was among the more
realistic Confederates, and in the early summer of 1861

he wrote to his sister-in-law to tell her that too many Southerners underestimated "the strength & vigilance of the North." His view was, and he charged Virginia Clay to let her husband know, that "our troops go into battle usually unequipped & undisciplined with every man resolving to live or die a hero . . . & it pains me to know how many will fall victims to their own valor & sense of security against yankee troops."[4]

It was not surprising that Virginia Clay should be taken into his confidence on important matters concerning the war. The world of public affairs was the milieu in which she had spent most of her adult years. Hers had been an easy life, and she had lived it fully in that pink-gauze atmosphere of the legendary "Old South." Born in 1825 in North Carolina, she lost her mother at an early age and her father sent her to Tuscaloosa to be raised by relatives in Alabama's little capital city. Here Virginia enjoyed a carefree childhood among many relatives and received the usual schooling offered females of that day. From time to time her father came for visits and on one occasion he took her to Mobile, where she acquired a liking for dancing, parties, and the theater. Immediately after finishing instruction at the Nashville Female Academy in Tennessee, she returned home and, while participating fully in Tuscaloosa's social life, married Clement C. Clay, Jr., the rising young legislator from Huntsville.[5]

Well born and well married, Virginia proved herself a valuable asset in promoting her husband's career when he was elected United States senator in 1853. At Washington this extraordinary woman's masterful personality and manifest special abilities established her as one of the foremost social leaders and she became a confidante to prominent national and sectional leaders of the 1850 decade. The "Belle of the Fifties" had a reign that was positively brilliant; one rival hostess admitted freely that she was "a woman of great vivacity, and rare charm of manner," whose "cleverness and wit made her a delightful companion."[6]

When Clay was elected to be Alabama's Confederate senator, Virginia transferred her social activities to Richmond, where she set up housekeeping in a small hotel suite and proceeded to play hostess to Southern politicians in the same grand manner as in antebellum Washington. Her reputation as a friend of powerful officials attracted much attention, and persons from all over the South sought her assistance in getting government patronage. It was a role she loved and she was doubtless well pleased when John A. Read dubbed her "the *Prime Minister* to your good husband, and one of the Extra Constitutional advisers of the President." The cagey Read was not being entirely hypocritical, but was merely recognizing that Virginia's influence could go a long way to help him obtain a munitions contract and also the adoption of an invention of his called a "Torpedo Ram."[7]

Requests for help came frequently and she was bombarded with a score of letters asking for her intercession in regard to a wide range of subjects. Leading the list by far were those pertaining to military appointments. James Holt Clanton, for example, requested the post of "a conscripting officer"[8] and Lieutenant W. P. Barnes asked for her help in getting him the rank of captain.[9] Women also solicited favors, but few were as candid as Euphradia Poeltnitz Johnson when she wrote asking for a surgeon's post for her brother-in-law. Virginia was reminded that her "acquaintance and influence with Mr. [Leroy P.] Walker, Secretary of War, might procure for him that office."[10]

Actually, Virginia Clay was more a part of the atmosphere than the substance of the power structure of the Confederate government. She had no specific assignments and she did not actively seek any official post. Men in high places liked her and many trusted her judgment on certain matters of state. On several occasions Lucius Q. C. Lamar used her as a sounding-board and critic in affairs involving his career as a diplomat. On his part, the Mississippian kept her posted on the course of foreign affairs and once sent a speech regarding Confederate relations with France[11] to her for her criticism. Domestic issues captured her attention too, and from time to time she registered mild opposition against certain actions of the Confederate government. For one thing, she questioned the heavy tax burden imposed on Southerners and predicted that if some relief were not forthcoming, "wearied citizens" would not be able "to sustain a further drain upon them."[12] Sharing the same opinion was Nannie Yulee, the wife of Florida's first United States senator and a close personal friend of Virginia's. Nannie, however, had stronger feelings on the matter and wrote to her friend "to use your influence to induce those petty and fancy law makers to come up to our necessities . . . and stop placing tax, tax, tax, on our people."[13]

Much of Mrs. Clay's influence stemmed from her warm bond of friendship with the Davis family. She was often a guest at the Confederate White House during the times she lived in Richmond, and she kept up a lively correspondence with the president while sojourning in other parts of the South. This correspondence suggests a close relationship unmatched in Davis's relations with other women of the Confederacy. At least he seemed to enjoy her company very much and did not hesitate to express keen disappointment on not being able to see her more often. "From day to day I have hoped to have been able to see you," he wrote in 1863, "but continued indisposition intervened to deprive me of the pleasure."[14] The chief executive became a source of consolation during Clay's absence on a Canadian mission. In a letter dated August 31, 1864, he sympathized with her desire to join Clay, but advised against it and went on to assure her that "his health has improved . . . and we hope that he will bring back increased ability to labor in the cause of the Confederacy. . . ."[15]

Yet Virginia would not take a negative answer, even from Davis, and she continued to pester him about her husband's welfare. Letters poured in to such an extent that her brother-in-law ordered her to stop because the president was "in a sea of troubles & has no time for thought of anything except the safety of the country."[16] Later, when the Confederacy was disintegrating, Major Hugh Lawson Clay used even more direct language and told his kinswoman to "move in the direction of Alabama. . . ."[17] When the end came, she fled to Macon, Georgia, where she placed herself under the protection of General Howell Cobb, a short time later to be joined by her husband. They remained in Georgia, along with a small group of Confederate notables, until captured by Northern authorities.

While other contemporaries of Mrs. Clay did not possess the advantage of operating near the center of power, many nevertheless harbored strong opinions regarding public affairs. The greater percentage of them, however, still hid behind anonymity when criticizing and advising Confederate leaders on political, economic, and military matters. But none could match Augusta J. Evans's involvement in the world of politics, even though she made no public appearances nor ever favored equal rights for women. Her chief gift was the written word, and she used words with telling effect on individual policy-makers as well as on public opinion.

When the war started, Augusta was twenty-six, unmarried, and the author of a best-selling novel, *Beulah*. It was the beginning of a new era for her and at first she neglected research and writing for such war work as nursing and sewing for soldiers. But physical effort alone proved unsatisfactory and it was not long before she again took up her pen to express her political philosophy and advise leading Southern officials on matters of public concern. As the war went on, Augusta developed her own ideas about the government the new nation should have. In a letter to Congressman Jabez L. M. Curry she told of losing what few illusions had lingered in her mind about entrusting power to the hands of the people. To her, popular sovereignty and universal suffrage not only fostered corruption and demagogism, but were the primary causes of the downfall of past republics. It was her conviction that only the elite should be allowed to vote and, consequently, "hopeless anarchy" would be avoided in the Confederacy.[18]

However, the Alabama writer was no heartless authoritarian, but a firm believer in fair play, and she quickly reacted unfavorably toward certain measures of the Confederate government. Especially galling was the Conscription Act of 1862, which permitted exemptions for those persons owning twenty or more slaves. This was

Montgomery street scene in 1861, showing women watching parade
(*Reproduced from* Harper's Illustrated Weekly)

Flag presentation, 1861, at LaGrange Military Academy (La-Grange, Alabama)
(*Courtesy Alabama Dept. of Archives and History*)

Aurelia Blassingame Fitzpatrick
Social leader of Richmond and Montgomery
(*Reproduced from Virginia Clay-Clopton*, A Belle of the Fifties)

Virginia Clay
Social leader for Confederate brass
(*Reproduced from Virginia Clay-Clopton*, A Belle of the Fifties)

Kate Cumming
Hospital matron with Army of Tennessee
(*Frontispiece from Kate Cumming, Gleanings from Southland*)

Myra Eulalie Knox Semmes
Richmond hostess
(*Reproduced from Thomas C. DeLeon,* Belles, Beaux and Brains of the 60's)

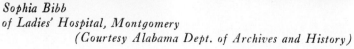

Sophia Bibb
of Ladies' Hospital, Montgomery
(*Courtesy Alabama Dept. of Archives and History*)

Anne Lewis Knox
Charter member of Ladies Aid Society of Montgomery
(Courtesy Alabama Dept. of Archives and History)

Augusta Jane Evans
Southern propagandist
(Courtesy Alabama Dept. of Archives and History)

Emma Sansom
Teenage heroine
    (Courtesy Alabama Dept. of Archives and History)

Juliet Opie Hopkins
Hospital founder and administrator
    (Courtesy Alabama Dept. of Archives and History)

Eliza McLane
Wilcox County nurse
      (Courtesy Dr. R. C. Kennedy, Camden, Alabama)

Alabama Confederate Belle (1861)
      (Courtesy Alabama Dept. of Archives and History)

Two unknown Alabama Confederate brothers in homespun uniforms
      (Courtesy Alabama Dept. of Archives and History)

First White House of the Confederacy
Montgomery, Alabama
        (Courtesy Alabama Dept. of Archives and History)

patently unfair, and in opposing exemptions she told
Curry that the Act was responsible for the "insubordination and disaffection which is rife in our armies." Moreover, inequalities in the administration of subsequent
draft acts aroused repeated comments from her and she
never failed to register strong objections with public
officials on the matter. She also championed the underdog
and opposed harsh punishment meted out to army de-
serters, who, in her opinion, had merely heeded "the cries
of hungry wives and starving children . . . unable to work
the fields or secure food and clothing." This biting,
trenchant critic also saw many demons in the practice of
holding secret sessions of Congress. If not discontinued,
she warned, any "unpopular measure would be . . . indis-
criminately heaped on all who chance to constitute our
Congress," and included Curry in this category.[19]

Augusta J. Evans took a keen interest in military affairs
and, although relying on newspaper accounts of battles
and occasional reports from General Beauregard and
others, she formulated definite opinions of her own regarding strategy. In 1861 she revealed herself as an advocate of aggressive action when she expressed deep disappointment that Confederate forces did not pursue "the
demoralized and panic-stricken" Federal armies after the
First Battle of Manassas. Instead of holding military
authorities responsible, she blamed the Confederate cabinet and especially "the evident timidity of President
Davis" for not allowing the Southern army to follow up
the victory. For this reason Augusta ruefully concluded
that the war was slated "to drag its slow length along,
possibly for years" because *our leaders lack nerve.*[20]

A year later in a letter to Curry she was positively
ebullient over the Southern victory at Fredericksburg.

Comparing it to the Battle of Leipzig of the Thirty Years' War, Augusta indulged freely in historical parallels. She wrote:

> Has it ever occurred to you, there is a parallelism between *McClelland and Wallenstein*. That Burnside is playing the role of *Tilly* and McClellan's speedy restoration to command, is Wallenstein-like, rendered more than probable by his late reversal.

This armchair general also found a further parallel in Stonewall Jackson as "a latter-day Gustavus Adolphus."[21] But the surrender of Vicksburg in 1863 left her so despondent that she compared herself to Mary Tudor of England over the loss of Calais. "When I am dead," she said, "it will be found engraved on my heart." Then with unrelenting fury she turned on General John Pemberton and accused him of either "treachery or stupidity" for failing to hold the Mississippi stronghold.[22]

Although Miss Evans condemned and admired in turn other high-ranking officers, no Confederate commander measured up to the stature of General Beauregard. She found no fault in any of his actions and considered all detractors as potential enemies of the war effort. Following his censure by Davis for involvement in the 1863 round robin against Braxton Bragg, she wrote her hero that his action "embodies the wishes of the entire Confederacy." To her Davis was wrong and his "systematic injustices . . . heaped upon you," makes "the blood *tingle* in my veins. . . ." She went on to assure him that she had had talks with Generals Sterling Price and Joseph Johnston and they both spoke "of *you* Sir, in terms of unmeasured admiration and exalted esteem. . . ."[23] Beauregard agreed in full with this estimate and, upon being slighted in a

speech by Davis at Charleston in 1863, unburdened the
most intimate feelings to his Mobile confidante. He let her
know that Davis had "done more than if he had thrust a
fratricidal dagger into my heart! He has *killed* my enthusiasm in our holy cause . . . ! May God forgive him—
I fear I shall not have charity enough to pardon him."[24]
Nor did Augusta have any "charity" either, since she had
already made up her mind that the general was "an illus-
trious victim of *Presidential Jealousy.* . . ."

While counseling with civil and military officials,
Augusta Evans was also writing articles for magazines
and letters to newspapers, which were designed to influence
public opinion on the issues of the day. In 1863, two years
before the end of the war, she published a novel entitled
Macaria: or, Altars of Sacrifice, which purported to explain the Confederate cause to Southerners and the
world. Despite the fact that she considered the work a
masterpiece, it did not come up to her past standards of
writing, but its one considerable achievement was to win
for her the reputation as the foremost propagandist of
the Confederacy. Reading it, a dedicated Southerner
could convince himself that history was undeniably on his
side, that all his sacrifices were worthwhile, all slave
owners humane and wise, and that all his enemies were
villainous. Outsiders were served a catalogue of benefi-
cent war aims that included the main eye-catcher of the
right of an oppressed people to revolution and independence. In short, the Confederacy was waging a war for the
preservation of the true republican form of government.[25]
Even though the book had a limited circulation, it was
declared "contraband and dangerous" by Federal General
George H. Thomas and it was banned in army camps
under his command.[26]

Many other articulate women opposed certain governmental measures that appeared unwise or downright hurtful to the future success of the Confederacy. To be sure, most did not move in the charmed circle of great policy-makers as did Mrs. Clay, nor did many possess the writing ability of Miss Evans; they nevertheless had strong opinions on matters of public concern. The most frequent grievances centered on conscription and wartime hardships. To Sarah Espy of Cherokee County, the 1862 draft was "as . . . shameful a one as Congress ever passed," not only on account of its exemption provisions, but mainly because the solons responsible for the act had raised their own salaries and yet, she noted, "the greater part of the time they are home attending to their businesses."

Nor did she look with favor upon the actions of conscription officers who took all men between the ages of eighteen and forty-five. Such a practice would result in a manpower drain in her community, and besides, many physically unfit men were forced into the army. In fact, she personally knew of one eighteen-year-old youth who had been ill "all of his days, and looks like death, but he has to go." Sarah predicted that if these conditions continued, "we shall sooner or later have a rebellion among ourselves."[27] Kate Cumming reflected the same disapproval and reported many cases in which men had been drafted after having been rejected by army doctors several times. This practice, she opined, was not only inhumane, but highly impractical since many rejectees had died before serving any time in the army.[28]

Some ventured opinions on strictly military affairs and a few seriously questioned the ability of military leaders, especially on matters involving the safety of kinsmen. In 1862, when Mrs. Dorian Hall of Lowndesboro learned that her son might be sent to Roanoke Island in Virginia at the precise time that he was up for discharge, she advised him to come home and counsel with her before considering reenlisting. She told him that the prospect of being stationed on an island "strikes terror in my soul," and went on to say that "our officers are so short-sighted as to place their men right into the hands of their enemy" without a chance of retreat, which made her "shudder." Once more, the concerned mother expressed her disappointment at Confederate reversals in Kentucky, for which she laid the blame squarely on inefficient leadership of the military.[29]

During the last year of the war an amazing number of the state's women came out with propositions for solving the Confederacy's financial problems. Although presented in a spirit of helpfulness, most were too impractical or ludicrous for serious consideration. Among the long list of proposals appearing in newspapers was the plan of "A Lady from Mobile" suggesting that Southern women donate the family jewels and silver "to assist in redeeming the currency of the Confederacy." If the amount proved insufficient for the purpose in mind, she recommended that monies derived from the sale of these valuables be divided "equally among our soldiers."[30] At the same time another Mobilian, signing herself as "Delilah, A Niece of James Madison," offered an even odder proposition for raising funds. The late president's relative proposed that all Southern women sell their hair to European wigmakers. In advancing the soundness of her idea, she explained that there were at least two million females with two braids of hair each, which could be sold at twenty dollars a pair and thus give $40,000,000 toward retiring the national debt. In calling for the biggest hair-cut in

Dixie, this naïve woman exhorted all over twelve years of age to: *Let every patriotic woman's head be shingled . . .* and even the vilest foe will stand abashed in her presence."[31]

The antebellum attitude regarding women's place in society carried over during the war years and the greater number remained mute in the face of the great events taking place around them. No doubt the silent majority had opinions on public issues at one time or another, but most considered themselves inadequately informed to advise public officials or offer master plans for saving the Confederacy-at-bay. But they did not shun the responsibility of acting as confidantes to relatives in the services. Quite predictably, the problems of nostalgia and getting out of the army led all others on which women were taken into confidence by the men in uniform. For example, Reuben Vaughn Kidd wrote home that he was completely "powerless to give expression to one-half the bitter loneliness, desolation and vacancy of feeling in my heart on leaving my native home."[32] Private Peel wrote along the same lines a short time after leaving for duty. He could think of nothing good about army life and was especially tired of eating mess-hall biscuits. If it were possible to come home, he confessed a willingness to eat biscuits even there, provided they were prepared by his mother.[33]

By 1863, Captain Horace M. Smith found the army unbearable and he began looking for an honorable way to get a discharge. The Northern-born commander of a Eufaula company reflected this desire in several letters to his wife and finally wrote that if it were "not for a law which requires the Brig. Genl. to immediately conscript any officer who is dismissed or resigns, I think I would resign at once" and come home. Smith, however, did not relish becoming a private, and he decided to remain in the service.[34] Experiencing the same agony of indecision was Joel D. Murphree of Troy, who also found the prospects of civilian status so alluring that he never failed to mention his desire to get out of the army in letters to his wife. For instance, on May 26, 1864, he wrote her that "it is my duty to serve the Confederacy in the army and at the same time I would like very well to have the pleasure of remaining at home with my family."[35] After several months of hard thinking on the subject, Murphree wrote that he would be willing to carry the mail near home free of charge if it meant a discharge from the army.[36] Although he never once acknowledged what Mrs. Murphree had to say about this plan, she was undoubtedly in full agreement with it. Murphree's plan fell through, and he and thousands of others continued to gripe about army life to their womenfolk until the very end of the war.

Frequently women were recipients of advice from the men at the front. Both prominent and ordinary soldiers had occasion for writing home on matters pertaining to the welfare of their families. Such correspondence intensified during periods of crisis on the home front and was just as frequent on the eve of big battles. The presence of Northern occupation forces in various parts of Alabama caused many men to become greatly concerned about the safety of female relatives. Some recommended a policy of aloofness and others advised that feminine heads of households obey all regulations even to the extent of taking the oath of allegiance to the United States. William C. McClelland went a step further and warned his sister never to marry a Northern soldier. "Why Matilda," he wrote, "a Yankee smells worst than a mink—how any Southern Lady can marry one of them I cant see to save my life."[37] Before going into action in east Tennessee in 1863, Major W. J. Mims wrote his wife the following advice in case of his death:

> You know my views about debts, etc. Be prudent & economical until you get out of debt then buy you a good conveyance, furnish our house well, have comfortable fixtures of every description, always remember the importance of educating our children . . . of impressing early upon the little girls the beauty of modesty, chastity & holiness and cultivate charity towards them, the servants & the world.

There was more. In the event of remarriage, Mims advised his wife against "a man of bad morals no matter what his position in society," but instead, get "an honest, sensible man and one of tried integrity."[38]

Some promised to become better husbands and provide a good life after the war. In 1862 during the heat of a Tennessee campaign, Dr. Phillips Fitzpatrick made such a vow and went on to say that he felt "right happy . . . when I think over all these things that are going to be, and I think that I have already the queen who is going to preside over this fairy castle." The doctor confessed his love and promised to read over this letter of fidelity at some future "rainy day" to remind him of his wartime pledges.[39] Others took wives into their confidence in efforts to vindicate their actions. In 1863 Raphael Semmes wrote his wife, then living with relatives in Ohio, "not to believe the malicious and false reports that you see in Northern newspapers." The commander of the C.S.S. Alabama felt compelled to remind her that his ship was "a well ordered and well-disciplined man-of-war, & I make war according to civilized rules, & with far more mercy than my enemy, and yet," he continued, "they abuse me in the public prints & call me a 'pirate'—a pirate because I am doing what they themselves are doing, destroying the enemy's property—no more."[40]

Alabama women were also kept abreast of the lighter and the tragic sides of army life. Many of the younger soldiers penned letters containing daring descriptions of bravery under fire and statements calculated to prove their manhood to doubting relatives. In 1861 Crenshaw Hall wrote to his sister after the First Battle of Manassas, in answer to her doubts concerning his ability to kill anyone, that it had "afforded me a good deal of pleasure to kill one of them." Hall ended his play at bravado by promising to send her "a little Yankee" for a servant as soon as one could be found alive.[41] Another member of the same family let a relative know that the letter dated October 22, 1863, had been written just a short distance from enemy lines and that their guns "could easily knock to pieces the tent" in which he was billeted. In describing the food Hall complained bitterly of having only cold fare, but being an enterprising soldier he took credit for inventing a dish called "cush," a soon-popular boiled mixture of bacon grease, chopped beef, corn bread, biscuit, and water. In a teasing way he predicted that Laura Hall would probably "turn up [her] nose" at this dish, but to a seasoned veteran such as himself it was "quite a luxury."[42]

Every aspect of army existence was forwarded to home-front relatives; even the gruesome details of battlefields were described by some eye-witnesses with a candor undreamed of in peacetime. For example, one young soldier wrote his mother that after one battle he "saw men with *faces,* arms, & *Legs,* mangled and torn in every shape" and that some of his comrades "couldn't look at them at all, & some became weak in the knees," but not he.[43] Yet, there was always the lighter side to be shared with the women back home. In this regard Harden Cochrane let his mother in on a humorous scandal that was making the rounds of an army camp. According to the gossip a high-ranking officer who had been an aide-de-camp of General Beauregard's was an inveterate wife-beater. As Cochrane understood the details, the man in question had married "a respectable lady" in Augusta, Georgia, and had brought her to Montgomery where he proceeded "to whip her nearly to death." Such conduct shocked the young soldier all the more because the officer appeared to him "like a most polished gentleman and . . . in every way respectable." Besides, he used "the most flowing language in conversation and claimed to be the son of the governor of Florida."[44]

While most men in gray derived a great deal of satisfaction in sharing experiences with their womenfolk, there were even more who wanted to hear about what was going on at the home front. It was a rare soldier who did not plead for more information and a rarer woman who ignored the request. In fact, some women went to extremes in filling letters with trivia and petty details about such subjects as housekeeping and the latest wedding. Regardless of content, the men continued to request more and more letters. For example, after spending some time in the company of Virginia and Celeste Clay in Macon, Georgia, Clifford and Sidney Lanier went to great lengths to keep in contact through an exchange of letters. Soon after leaving for Virginia the two budding members of the literati mentioned how much they enjoyed the carefree life of the Georgia town and requested their former hostesses to supply them with news of the happenings there. Later on,

Clifford appeared to be practicing his writing skills on the Clay women. He recorded his feelings about having to leave for the battlefields with:

> What a transition is this—from the Spring and peace of Macon, to this muddy and war-distressed country! Going to sleep in the moonlight and soft air of Italy, I seem to have waked imbedded in Lapland snow.

And in an irrelevant passage he waxed even more eloquent:

> Yet, as I would not be an Anthony, with genius bold, and confident in Egypt, but a trembler and white-livered, in the presence of Octavious at Rome, I summon all my heroism, doff that which became me when environed by flowers, poetry, music and blooming maidens, and don shield and mail . . . prepared to resist ruder shocks than those of love's arrows.

In closing, he asked the Clay women to "throw a ray through this darkness, show . . . one glimpse of the blue sky through all this battle-smoke, write to us. . . ."[45]

But there was no ray through the darkness for all too many Alabama women who received death notices. One notice was sent to Mrs. J. D. Cadenhead of Barbour County, recounting the death of her husband in the following terse lines:

> Sister it becomes my painful duty to inform you that Mr. Cadenhead is no more. He was killed yesterday, in a charge on the enemy. I do not know where he was struck, but from what I can learn he was shot through the chest with a minie ball. I saw him lying in the field but we were retreating and there was no time for me to

examine him further than to see that he was dead. His body was left in the hands of the enemy.[46]

The informant closed with an expression of personal sympathy for the new widow and assured her that ultimate Confederate victory would be a source of consolation in the future.

5

. . . the whirr of the spinning wheel was heard
from morning until night.

On the evening of September 1, 1862, Martha Jane
Crossley of Perote, Alabama, broke her usual habit
of retiring at an early hour. She knew that sleep would
not come easily, for she suffered from "a considerable
headache" brought on by a hard day's work making
clothing for a local military unit. Rather than endure the
agony of insomnia, this charter member of the Perote
Ladies' Aid Society whiled away the time by writing in
her diary. As she wrote of seeing poorly clad conscripts
passing through the village early that morning, the importance of her work took on greater meaning than ever before and she resolved to labor harder the following day.
With this renewal of purpose, her headache disappeared
and she began making preparations for retiring, but not
before expressing the wish to supply all soldiers with "the
little comforts the government does not furnish them."[1] A
large order, to be sure, but it reflected the ambition of
many members of those aid societies that were dedicated
to providing various articles of clothing for Confederate
soldiers.

Shortly after the outbreak of the war Alabama women
gathered in private residences, churches, and public halls

to lay plans for providing clothing for the soldiers. Within weeks women's aid societies sprang up in every county, until by January 1, 1862, there were over one hundred organizations hard at work spinning, weaving, sewing, and knitting military apparel of every description.[2] Such activity not only offered women the opportunity for making a worthwhile contribution to the war effort, but at the same time enabled them to engage in an exclusively feminine occupation without incurring serious public objections. It was also a chance for self-expression free of masculine competition and, in fact, attracted more volunteers than any other aspect of the war effort. For four long years thousands of Alabama Penelopes toiled ceaselessly with little or no recognition or reward except the personal satisfaction derived from knowing that they were assisting the Confederate cause.

In nearly every case, church leaders took an active part in stimulating the formation of auxiliary associations. Many a Sunday School teacher and missionary society president drew heavily from their memberships in establishing patriotic sewing circles. However, most women of a specific congregation organized these projects independently of any religious body, but made frequent use of church buildings for meeting places and as headquarters for recruiting drives. For example, on May 4, 1861, a group of lay women of a Montgomery Methodist Church announced the formation of an aid society and invited volunteers from every Christian denomination to meet with them in the church basement.[3] Here was founded the Ladies' Aid Association of Montgomery, which later won local fame as the largest and most productive organization of its kind in the capital city. Across town Caroline Hausman made use of the Synagogue in marshalling Jew-

ish women into the Hebrew Ladies Soldiers' Aid Society.[4]
A similar organization came into being at Mobile, which
was ready to supply clothing or money to outfit local servicemen from the port city.[5]

Thus Christians and Jews labored separately to help supply those "little comforts" that had been the ardent wish of
Miss Crossley in her small society at Perote. To make this
possible, Alabama's women created a structure of organization that approximated a minuscule government. Con-
stitutions were written providing for presidents, vice presidents, secretaries, and treasury officers, and in larger
societies boards of trustees were set up to coordinate over-
all activities. Some urban associations created male auxiliary committees composed of businessmen entrusted with
powers to act as bursars and to handle public relations.

Oftentimes presidents delivered inaugural speeches upon
assuming office. Speaking in behalf of the Ebenezer Society
of Bibb County, Emilie Lanning pledged her group "to do
all they can, for the Government, the soldiers, and the
county." She also went on to say that "To talk about sub-
jugating such a people as the Southern people is not only
madness; it is consummate folly!"[6] Caroline Hausman
spoke along the same lines, but also wrote the governor
that her group was deeply involved "in this gigantic struggle for liberty and self-government, and with the help of
the Being above we hope to see soon victory perched
upon our banners and peace once more restored to our
glorious Confederacy."[7]

At the outset these societies concentrated on supplying
only local and state soldiers; with few exceptions this
policy continued until the close of the war. Community
pride was especially strong among small town and rural
organizations, where members went all out to make sure

that the local warriors were properly clad. It was this spirit which moved the Conecuh County Aid Society "to knit socks, make cloth, buy cloth, and make it up into uniforms for county companies."[8] Several Selma organizations, working independently of each other, produced thousands of garments for home town service men.[9] Similarly, the women of an Opelika group joined forces with the students of a local female academy and turned out a sufficient number of uniforms to outfit every member of the Opelika True Volunteers.[10]

While most women affiliated with an organization, there were a few who preferred to work alone. This was the case of Mrs. William Collins of Auburn when she offered to make one hundred uniforms free of charge for any Lee County unit.[11] Quite often members took the personal responsibility of performing extra work. When Annie Strudwick of Demopolis was not teaching or working with the local aid society, she traveled to neighboring towns begging merchants for socks and other wearing apparel. This one-woman campaign was successful and she frequently returned laden with ready-made supplies for local soldiers.[12]

In rural sections where the population was small and scattered over wide areas, it was impractical to organize aid societies. Yet many women living in isolated communities undertook to provide clothing as an individual enterprise and sometimes combined their efforts in informal community projects. When Fannie Beers visited Alabama relatives after a tour of duty in Richmond hospitals, she took note of one such activity in the Black Belt. The hospital matron was pleased to discover that "looms were set up on every plantation," and "the whirr of the spinning wheel was heard from morning until night." She also reported seeing slaves "hovering over large cauldrons, continually thrusting down into the boiling dye the products of the looms, to be transformed into Confederate gray or *butternut jeans.*" Many wide halls of plantation houses were crowded with "tables piled with the newly dyed cloth and hanks of woolen or cotton yarn." It seemed to her that "the knitting of socks went on incessantly"—many women working all day and continuing their labors at night by the light of pine knots. When a sufficient number of articles were finished, a meeting was held in a nearby church where the women brought their goods, helped pack them, and then forwarded the parcels to the men at "the front."[13]

In even remoter sections, such as in southeastern Alabama, the manufacture of soldiers' clothing became strictly a family undertaking. After the war Mary Love Fleming told of such a project among her people in Dale County. Members of the family gathered on a rotation basis in their homes, where they made "uniforms, socks, and gloves, etc." for their respective relatives. Even the children were pressed into duty as nonperishable foods and other items were prepared for shipment to the Virginia camps. When a specified amount was ready, an elderly male member of the family or a local soldier returning to duty after a furlough was deputized to take the supplies to their destination.[14]

The operation of formal organizations were much the same in all areas of the state. Typical of the scope and output of small societies was the one at Perote. According to the group's secretary, Martha Jane Crossley, the young women were taught to spin and weave by elder members whose skills went back to pioneer times. A regular work schedule was set up by officers, with each member assigned a specific task to perform. Some made caps, others worked on gloves, underclothes, and towels, while still others prepared boxes of food or other gifts. From time to time cherished items of clothing were donated to be cut up into functional garments. Miss Crossley opined that such sacrifices were always cheerfully given, since she was certain the donor knew that "the poor soldiers . . . fighting for us will be made more comfortable."[15]

The project of furnishing clothing for local men was taken up with no less enthusiasm by the highly organized and efficient Mobile Military Aid Society. Founded on May 3, 1861, under the leadership of Ellen S. Walker and Adelaide deVendel Chaudron, this group soon fulfilled its original purpose and was ready to offer its services "to any Alabama Company in the Confederate Army." However, it became necessary for them to charge for their work and the necessary material. They offered to make uniforms at $2.00 each, "a pair of drawers at 20¢ each, Hickory shirts at 25¢ each, and overshirts with pockets at 30¢ each."[16] Prospective customers were allowed to select color schemes and the quality of the material to be used. If purchased from the society's stores, material could be had at wholesale prices. In addition, these enterprising women offered to knit 3,500 pairs of socks at $4.50 a dozen for any company serving the Confederacy.

During the early months of the war no official steps were taken to coordinate the efforts of Alabama's aid societies. But as the first winter approached, Governor A. B. Moore issued an appeal for cold weather garments. He specifically asked those engaged in supplying clothes to begin work on "woolen uniforms, flannel shirts, wool socks and blankets."[17] At the same time the Probate Judge of each community were ordered to act as receiving agents and to keep detailed records of those items which the aid societies deposited in their offices. These officials were also empowered to ship supplies to Montgomery or Mobile at government expense. Similar appeals were issued in succeeding years and each time aid members attempted to comply with the governor's request. Members everywhere raided trunks long neglected in attics or store rooms for wool remnants while others busily began knitting socks and other warm clothing. Some cut up carpets for blankets and a few organizations made public appeals for the donation of wool yarn. Women everywhere set to work immediately knitting socks. They were seen plying their needles furiously at social functions, while riding in wagons or carriages, and even during church services. A Mobile group offered "to knit up" as much wool yarn as the public could supply to its members.[18]

A sock-knitting mania swept the state and became the *raison d'être* for nearly every aid society. Judging from the output of this article, it would appear that every Alabama soldier was well supplied with warm socks, if nothing else. Socks poured in from all quarters. For example, the Montgomery Hebrew Society contributed 114 pairs[19] and a Mobile association sent in a total of 1,200 pairs along with the statement that "many willing fingers are now diligently plying their needles to furnish more of the much needed socks."[20] The president of the Hopewell Aid Society at Cokersville wrote the governor that she had recently ordered her members to concentrate exclusively on socks and would continue doing so until further orders were received to the contrary.[21]

Most sewing societies also contributed great varieties of food, toilet articles, and other small luxury items. Contemporary accounts abound with long lists of preserves, dried fruits, and cakes sent to men serving in far-away

battle stations. It was not uncommon for these recipients
to open boxes from home containing an imposing array of
reading material together with alcoholic beverages carefully packed in syrup buckets. But, as the war progressed,
sewing groups also were called upon to contribute much-
needed hospital supplies. Urgent appeals began coming
soon after the men left for duty, and then intensified after
the first battles were fought. On December 21, 1961, Opie
Hopkins, the head of Alabama hospitals in Richmond,
published an appeal in the state's newspapers for hospital
stores ranging from mattresses to bandages. Especially
critical was the need for soap, and she included a simple
recipe that could easily be followed in the home manufacture of this item.[22] Emergency calls for help came from
time to time to those societies located nearest the battle
zones. For example, during the Shiloh campaign in 1862,
the medical officer of the Twenty-Eighth Alabama Regiment addressed the societies of Greene, Perry, Dallas,
Bibb, Shelby, and Jefferson counties for such supplies as
pillows, bed linens, and foodstuffs.[23]

Before the end of 1861 many sewing circles either diversified their services or converted entirely to producing
hospital supplies. One of the first to make a complete trans-
formation was the Selma Aid Association, when its members voted on June 1, 1861, to abandon the manufacture
of clothing for the production of linens and bandages for
those hospitals catering to Alabamians "at the seat of war
in Virginia."[24] Others followed in short order and women's
groups, usually bearing the name "Ladies' Hospital Aid
Society," came into being in nearly every county.

Similar to sewing circles, these organizations were usually allied with religious denominations and the most effec-
tive organizations were confined mainly to urban areas. For

instance, the pastor of a Florence Presbyterian Church supplied the incentive for the formation of a hospital association in the north Alabama city. While in process of delivering his sermon one Sunday morning in June of 1861, this minister suddenly abandoned his text and began urging the women to organize a society to make "bandages, lint, etc." for Confederate hospitals. The manse was offered as a meeting place and that evening swarms of women appeared for work. Present were "ladies of all ages, from aged matrons and Mothers in Israel down to the Miss in her teens." Among them was "old Mrs. John Coffee," who gave instructions in rolling bandages "as she did in the days of yore when her gallant husband helped Old Hickory . . . repel the British from our borders" in the War of 1812. Glowing with satisfaction, the minister reported that it was "incredible to see how much was done in a few hours by fair hands and patriotic hearts."[25]

The same spirit animated Mobile women, and several hospital societies took form there during the war years. In addition to the Mobile Military Aid Society, there was the Soldiers' Friend Society, organized for the lofty purpose of providing "relief and comfort for sick and wounded soldiers" undergoing treatment at the Moore Hospital.[26] Still another organization, with the less dramatic name of Ladies' Supply Society, was established in 1862 to furnish "the sick and convalescent soldiers with nourishment . . . not supplied by the military" at the Marine Hospital. During the first year of operation its members visited patients, gave them food, and a few volunteered as practical nurses for over 6,000 patients. Others cleaned floors, made beds, and labored at those undramatic, but necessary, chores connected with the hospital's operation. For these services they received the highest praise from Dr. J. C. Nott, the Medical Director of the Mobile division. In an annual report he declared the hospitals under their care to be "as clean as a parlor," and besides, they had "furnished in abundance" all the delicacies "craved by the sick inmates."[27]

Alabama women were especially quick in responding to movements designed to produce materials of war and the construction of gunboats. Early in 1861, the restless energies of Augusta J. Evans found an outlet in helping to manufacture sandbags for Fort Morgan in Mobile Bay. After a week's work the indefatigable patriot and her group were able to present military authorities with over 900 bags.[28] Simultaneously with this project came an offer from the sales representative of the Grover Baker Sewing Machine Company to make "upwards of a hundred bags a week."[29] At rare intervals men ineligible for the army were pressed into the services of aid societies. On July 25, 1861, the Montgomery Ladies' Aid Association publicly announced that those men who visited them during working hours would be put to work covering canteens. However, the newspaper carrying the announcement thought this a bit too risky and expressed the hope that "no Buckeye juice" would be put into canteens destined for soldiers.[30]

As in every Confederate state, the mania for constructing gunboats struck Alabama and during the spring of 1862 one such project was initiated by the women of Selma. Here was formed the Ladies' Gunboat Society with the specific purpose of raising funds to build a boat "for the defense of our Alabama coast." It was this group's avowed intention to be completely independent of men in this endeavor, since in their opinion

There is a stubborn, mulish proclivity inseparable from the masculine gender; and were it not for the smiles and tears and entreaties of lovely women, who alone have access to the iron boxes of our lords of creation, not a thing could be done, nor a boat could be built.

Consequently. they called only upon women for help and then the vessel would truly become a "monument to the industry, zeal, and devotion of the women of Alabama."[31]

This project elicited the support of hundreds of women from all walks of life and small amounts of money began coming in from every section of the state. It was such an attractive proposition that one little girl named Sallie Nichols of Summerfield gave half of her ten-dollar annual allowance toward the cost of construction. Moreover, Sallie considered her sacrifice worthwhile and far nobler than spending the money for "nick-nacks."[32] A group from Evergreen donated sixty dollars; the list of donors included a slave, Leanthia, whose contribution of one dollar constituted her only cash holdings.[33] "Wishing to aid my counttry in every way," wrote a soldier's wife, when she sent in a box of jewelry for the gunboat fund.[34] Despite the enthusiastic efforts, the movement failed for lack of sufficient funds. However, all monies on hand were donated to military hospitals containing Alabama service men located in the vicinity of Corinth, Mississippi.[35]

The Civil War imposed heavy demands upon women to perform endless deeds of charity on behalf of indigent dependents of the state's service men. While scores of unfortunates received some kind of government assistance, there were countless others supported through the personal charity of thousands of Alabama's more fortunate women. But, as the numbers began to increase, philanthropic organizations composed exclusively of women came into existence in Mobile and Montgomery. The first to go into action was the already heavily burdened Mobile Ladies' Military Aid Society. In 1862, in addition to its sewing and hospital projects, this group took on the responsibility of providing clothing and sustenance for the local families of soldiers who were unable to support themselves.[36] For over a year they carried on alone, supplying all kinds of clothing and foodstuffs out of their own resources, but they were finally forced to ask the governor for financial assistance.[37]

The members of another group, which was founded by Laura Pillard of Mobile in 1862, dedicated themselves to a similar purpose. This organization, however, was not diversified, but concentrated its efforts only on supplying clothing for the needy children of soldiers. In less than six months this society contributed enough garments to clothe 920 minors of the city and county. And they, too, requested state aid to be able to continue their operations.[38] Still another, under the name of the Female Benevolent Society, took care of war widows and their children. Led by Ellen S. Walker and drawing support entirely from private donations, these women purchased an old building to house their charges and it soon came to be known locally as "Widows' Row." After one journalist visited it, he reported finding twelve widows and six children living there; all appeared suitably clothed and "looked well fed."[39]

Societies of a similar nature were set up in Montgomery. Among the most enthusiastic and enduring was that of the Ladies' Benevolent Society, which had the lofty aim of doing whatever was necessary in helping "the poor of this place whether they be soldiers' wives or widows . . . suffer-

ing for want of daily food. . . ." Starting with a capital of
three hundred dollars gathered from members, it made
significant contributions to the relief of the poor of the
capital city. Frequent appeals for funds appeared in the
press and on one occasion they stressed the fact that if
donations failed to come in they would have to suspend
operations.[40] Although public gifts of money were meager,
they received enormous amounts of supplies-in-kind.

Before taking their case to the people for financial assistance nearly every one of the women's auxiliaries con-
fidently expected to become self-sufficient. Upon assuming
office as head of the Mobile Military Aid Society, President Ellen S. Walker announced the policy of living on
their own, of supplying all articles needed for healthy as
well as disabled soldiers from dues collected from the
membership. She reasoned that such a policy was economically sound and, besides, it was "a good way to save
money for our government" and at the same time "do
something for our brothers, husbands, and friends now
gone or going to the war."[41] The head of the Pine Flat and
River Beats' Soldiers' Aid Society of Dallas County expressed the same view when she reported, on August 20,
1861, having produced "from lint to cloth" twenty blankets for local soldiers.[42] Others met expenses from the
sale of "fancy sewing articles" or from monies derived
from amateur plays and tableaux vivants. From such
sources the members of a Notasulga society were able to
make "125 uniforms, 75 pairs of socks, 2 large boxes of
comforts," containing quilts, pillows, sheets, towels, dried
fruit, and wine for their relatives in the army.[43]

Despite attempts at financial independence, the infinite
demands for more and more supplies caught up with aid
societies until they were forced to seek public aid. Pub-

lishing messages with evangelistic fervor, they besought all Alabamians to give until it hurt. The responses were often generous and money and supplies began coming in from all quarters. Long lists of donations, containing a wide assortment of gifts, regularly appeared in the newspapers. For example, George Hails of Montgomery gave one local aid group two bales of cotton and a H. F. Stickney mailed a $100 Confederate bill to the governor with the stipulation that he give it "to the Society . . . within Alabama, which . . . is most effective in administering to the wants of soldiers."[44] The chief executive selected the Mobile Military Aid Society as the one best fulfilling the criterion of the donor.[45] Incalculable amounts of supplies were donated by individual families—some gave livestock, vegetables in season, and one woman even donated her husband's hair piece for a bald-headed soldier.[46] And so it went, until supplies ran out or invasion dried up public sources of help.

State government stores were also given to aid societies. In response to pleas from small organizations in the fall of 1861, Governor A. B. Moore inaugurated a system of help that was followed throughout the war. This policy called for furnishing sewing circles with such raw materials as were needed in the manufacture of clothing from the quartermaster general's depots at Montgomery or Mobile. A sampling of the large amounts made available included such items as "one bale of osnaburg with patterns and buttons, thread and hooks for making Great Coats" to the Havana, Alabama Soldiers' Aid Society.[47] "Enough material to make 100 jackets and pants to match" was sent to the Troy Ladies' Aid Society.[48] The quartermaster general at Montgomery was also instructed to give "375 yards of cotton cloth and like amount of linen to make Great

Coats and cloth lining" for the use of the Soldiers' Aid Society at Huntsville.[49]

Besides furnishing raw materials, the state also gave small amounts of public funds for the manufacture of specific articles of clothing. In 1862, for example, the governor decreed the payment of fifty cents and seventy-five cents respectively for each pair of heavy cotton and wool socks.[50] This pay scale applied equally to those who were not members of an organization and continued in force until the close of the war. No direct appropriations were made available to sewing groups, but those concerned with hospital work received generous amounts of public monies. Between 1861 and 1864 the legislature appropriated a total of $109,000 for the Mobile, Montgomery, Selma, and Huntsville hospital associations.[51] Out of this amount the Mobile Military Aid Society received the lion's share of $54,000 for its hospital services.

Unfortunately, no public funds per se were provided for those organizations devoted to the care of indigent persons. However, the Mobile Military Aid Society was permitted to use small amounts of state monies given to them for helping soldiers' families. In answer to letters from numerous persons asking for assistance, the Civil War governor usually expressed best wishes for success and explained that Alabama's economy was too weak for a full scale "war on poverty" outside of the official agencies already established for poor relief. Nevertheless, charitable groups persisted in operating on their own resources, and although substantial amounts came from private donations, they were never sufficient to meet the ever-growing need. Although it is impossible to determine the exact amounts collected, at least one observer estimated that it was greater than that provided by official sources.[52]

Women's auxiliaries were also confronted with problems other than financial. Not the least of these was the loss of goods en route to their destination. Frequent complaints reached the governor's office that the products of a certain organization had fallen into the hands of speculators and were being sold on the black market at exorbitant prices.[53] Some members grew tired of work and others became apathetic as the war stretched on into years. Petty jealousies and personality clashes among members accounted for the serious interruption of production and even caused some societies to disband altogether. There were also rare cases of larceny in which a trusted member appropriated goods for selfish reasons. In 1862 President Rebecca Dennis of the Antioch Ladies' Aid Society in Coosa County reported that one member had taken uniforms to Montgomery, where she sold them for $241.15 and sent the money to her son in Virginia.[54] After some attempt was made to locate the guilty party, the search was abandoned with the philosophic conclusion that she had apparently "flown the coop for good."[55]

Be that as it may, the task women set for themselves was actually too big for them to handle. It was, in fact, too big for the state and Confederate governments. Toward the end of the war official and private citizens came face to face with the reality that good intentions and high hopes for success are commendable attributes, but they seldom pick up the bill. In many ways it was a superb failure, which was realized by precious few of those involved in the aid societies until defeat encompassed all of them. Nevertheless, much of what they did for the war effort represented a genuine sacrifice on the part of individuals who, though failing in their purpose, continued working until the end. No doubt many found strength and inspiration from the paeans of praise heaped upon them by grateful soldiers. Among the many letters to the aid groups, the one from Private Willie Kyle to the Montgomery Ladies' Aid Association probably best expressed the gratitude felt by the service men. After extending his "heart-felt thanks for the valuable gifts and kindness" from Montgomery ladies, he went on to say that they and others of similar organizations were doing as much for the Confederate cause as the men in uniform to help to "free our soil from the tread of the invader and purchasing once more a peaceful and happy land."[56]

6

We cannot fight, so we must care for those who do.

At first many Alabama women viewed the Civil War as a grand pageant composed of handsome officers, brave young soldiers nattily attired in gray jackets embellished with brass buttons, waving flags, patriotic music, and inspirational speeches predicting an easy victory. The farthest thing from most people's minds was the prospect of anyone's getting seriously hurt. Certainly no one would get killed. After all, Yankees were no match for the invincible Southern warriors. The war could last only a few months, a year at most, and then the returning victors, barely disheveled, would stage an even grander pageant for the hosts of feminine admirers. All too many in authority shared this optimism, and when battles produced the inevitable casualties every level of government was caught short in providing adequate hospital facilities for sick and wounded soldiers.

This unexpected development was not the least of the problems facing the Civil War generation. Their war was fought in the "very last days of the medical Middle Ages," and inadequately trained doctors could only "meet the gigantic problems of military medicine and surgery with such means as they could command."[1] An even greater deficiency was felt in the field of nursing, for this profession had not attained the status of a specialized occupation requiring intensive training and practice. In fact, it had been less than a decade since Florence Nightingale employed women nurses during the Crimean War, and schools for the training of nurses were still in the primary stages of development. In 1861 the only women in the South possessing a modicum of nursing experience under controlled conditions were the Roman Catholic Sisters of Charity. Fortunately for Alabama, this religious order had two hospitals at Mobile that could be used for army patients, and soon after hostilities began they founded another in Montgomery for the exclusive use of military personnel. These establishments continued in operation until the end of the war.[2]

The realization that sick and wounded men required attention caused scores of patriotic lay women to defy convention and offer their services as volunteer nurses. Such a decision represented real courage on their part, since none had any experience beyond tending to members of their families and that pharmaceutical knowledge gained from the application of home remedies. Nor could any have had the remotest idea of the mental and physical hardships that awaited them, to say nothing of the lamentable working conditions brought on by the absence of a sophisticated medical corps.

But, like everything else connected with the war effort, those feminine noncombatants ignored the impossible. It was, for the truly dedicated a call for goodness, a "woman's mission . . . to soothe, to bind up, and to heal . . . the soldiers of our Southern Army," as Mrs. C. E. Trueheart saw it when she wrote the governor on June 20, 1861, offering to do these things. She was, moreover, pre-

pared to devote her "time, energy, strength & if necessary my life to the alleviation of the suffering of those who
have left homes, & their all for their country."[3] All she
required was the information where to go so that her
services could be put to maximum use.

Actually, Mrs. Trueheart had a wide choice of places.
There were the Richmond hospitals, the medical services
of the Army of Tennessee, or she could remain at home
and nurse in any one of the many medical facilities being
set up to care for disabled soldiers. Most women preferred the latter alternative and many eager women took
the lead in establishing organizations to expedite the creation of community hospitals. Among the first was the
Ladies' Hospital Association, founded in the Spring of
1861 at Montgomery. Like the sewing societies, it was
efficiently organized with officers and committees, and
each member was assigned a specific task such as rolling
bandages, preparing dietary foods, or obtaining necessary
supplies. Shortly after its founding, this organization converted two cottages, which had been donated by a Dr.
Carnot Bellinger, into a "Soldiers' Home" for treating
convalescent military patients. Appropriately, Mrs. Bellinger was named president and a Mrs. Walton was employed as a practical nurse. When a replacement could
not be found after Mrs. Walton's death, the members
took turns as volunteer nurses.[4] This establishment offered
an oasis of creature comforts for hundreds of less seriously
ill soldiers and continued in operation for the remainder
of the war.

In less than a year the Soldiers' Home proved inadequate, but instead of abandoning the project, the society
voted to enlarge its responsibilities and established a full-
scale hospital near the center of town. The new quarters

consisted of a three-story building and was dubbed the Ladies' Hospital of Montgomery. Sophia Gilmer Bibb, the Georgia-born wife of a prominent Alabama judge, was elected as head of the two facilities, a post she held throughout the war years. When Mrs. Bibb took charge at the age of sixty,[5] she brought into existence a new era of vigorous administration.

Among her outstanding innovations was that of getting local aid societies to contribute supplies of hospital stores. To facilitate this plan further she had space set aside at the hospital as a work room, to ensure a steady flow of goods on the spot and at the same time to furnish a pool of potential nurses in case of an emergency.[6] "Aunt Sophie," as she was affectionately called by friends, also took charge of many unpleasant tasks not specifically required of her office. Along this line she was especially diligent in overseeing the grisly task of burying dead patients. She was frequently seen in her carriage heading for the cemetery to supervise this melancholy function, and she is credited with managing funeral services for over eight hundred men.[7]

The Ladies' Hospital soon won widespread fame as one of the best health establishments in the state. Unsolicited tributes came in from persons in all ranks of life. A legislator from Bibb County was quite typical of these when he wrote of being convinced that many "a poor fellow has yet a lease on life that . . . would have died . . . but for the motherly attention they received from the kindhearted ladies that make it their business to wait on them as though they were their own children."[8] Indeed, its reputation was so well established that when the Confederate Medical Department assumed control over all hospitals in 1862, the Ladies' Hospital Association was permitted to remain in control of many administrative functions.[9] Medical authorities also consulted Mrs. Bibb and her assistant, Mrs. William Bell, in the selection of surgeons and other hospital personnel.[10]

Aunt Sophie was constantly confronted with financial problems, and although the Confederacy furnished enormous amounts of supplies, this did not satisfy the needs of the ever-growing number of patients. When private donations proved inadequate, she took her case to the legislature and succeeded in obtaining $20,000 from that source.[11] She once appealed to Jefferson Davis for permission to draw supplies from government stores in Montgomery. In granting permission the president paid her society the highest kind of praise when he wrote:

> The surgeon-general has informed me that the ladies' hospital is the best managed and most comfortable one in the Confederacy, and I will take pleasure in giving you a *carte blanc* for anything that may be necessary.[12]

No one denied Sophia Bibb's patriotism, but she never let her feelings stand in the way of admitting wounded Federal soldiers. When she was criticized for taking in a small number of prisoners of war, she merely explained that "they were suffering men and shall be made as comfortable as our Confederate soldiers."[13] This *beau geste* was slated to pay future dividends for the intrepid hospital administrator. When Federal forces captured Montgomery in 1865, the commanding general placed a guard at her home to protect her from molestation from stragglers after the main body of troops had left the city. Following the war, she became a leader in organizations set up to provide monuments for the Confederate war dead. She was elected as head of the Ladies' Memorial Association and served in that capacity until her death on January 11, 1887.[14]

Montgomery soon became an important medical center and by 1864 there were, in addition to the Ladies' Hospital, five other establishments. Among the largest, with 325 beds, was St. Mary's, which was founded by the Sisters of Charity, and it constituted the second feminine-run hospital in the capital city. Here five nuns supervised a large staff of stewards, laundresses, and slave orderlies. During emergencies the sisters themselves helped in every department by day and spent sleepless nights nursing in the crowded wards. Oftentimes space had to be found for over 500 patients, some even spilling over into the nuns' quarters. Yet, according to an 1864 medical inspector's report, St. Mary's came nearest to meeting the exacting requirements of a military hospital of any in the city. This official wrote that it was like all those he had seen operated by members of this religious order in other parts of the South: "Neatness, cleanliness & order characterize their presence everywhere."[15]

Alabama women were also active in establishing "Wayside Homes" for comfort of transient soldiers or for the care of those recuperating from illnesses. Nearly every county seat had one such institution where the men might rest, obtain hot meals, and, if sick, secure the necessary medicines and nursing services. A few women were known to equip health facilities and endow them with funds out of their own pockets. Moved by compassion and intense patriotism, Augusta J. Evans established a convalescent home on the grounds of her country estate near Mobile. According to her own account, she spent many "a sleepless vigil by day and night . . . sitting beside one whose life hung upon a slender thread for many days."[16]

Others who were tied down with housekeeping occasionally accepted one or two sick soldiers into their homes because they were either convalescent or hopeless cases. Some took in those with contagious diseases at great risk to members of their families. Mrs. Ellen G. McCloud of Albertville once nursed a typhoid fever victim, although she had two small children living in the same house. In explaining her reasons she merely wrote that "he was a soldier that needed attention." Moreover, when he was fully recovered she gave him "a good suit of gray jeans and some money to pay his fare home."[17] Many an aristocrat such as Virginia Clay specialized in caring for officers. While visiting friends at Columbus, Georgia, in 1864 she helped her hostess treat a young captain for gangrene, and when he showed signs of recovering entertained him with "merry talk" and carriage rides through the countryside.[18]

Individual efforts, however, were hardly adequate for the great numbers of military personnel stationed in and sent to such places as Mobile for treatment. Here the situation demanded cooperative effort if the job was to be done adequately. The most useful work along this line was performed by the Mobile Military Aid Society. Instead of establishing hospitals, this group pro-rated their members and funds among military hospitals already in existence in the city.[19] Some idea of the nature and scope of their work was witnessed by the Reverend C. F. Sturgis when he visited his son at Branch Hospital Number One. He wrote of seeing "ladies of the highest social position washing the sick soldiers' faces and hands, combing their hair, changing their beds, and bathing their fevered brows." This was enough to convince Sturgis that the patients "must almost imagine that they are at home," since they were getting the same kind of care expected from "their own loved mothers and sisters."[20]

As battles were fought near the borders of Alabama the multi-purpose Mobile society took on even greater responsibilities. During the Shiloh Campaign in 1862 an attempt was made to set up an "ambulatory Alabama Hospital" for the purpose of following the Army of Tennessee "in all its movements." Harriet Woodall, a member of the group's executive committee, was placed in charge of the project, but when she arrived a Corinth, Mississippi, military authorities withheld permission for carrying out the plan. Instead, Mrs. Woodall was given control of a hospital at Okolona, Mississippi, with the understanding that Alabama troops would be sent there for treatment. Simultaneously with these developments the parent organization obtained a warehouse near the depot at Mobile and proceeded to outfit it as a first aid station for disabled men shipped into the city. They employed a surgeon for the seriously ill, and while some members helped out as nurses, others met incoming trains to carry patients either to the warehouse or to military hospitals. For the convenience of those able to walk, placards were hung in the depot containing the addresses of various soldiers' rest homes and of citizens willing to take in convalescent cases.[21]

The Shiloh campaign also aroused into immediate action women's associations in western Alabama. A flurry of unaccustomed excitement permeated a string of communities stretching from Florence in northeastern Alabama to Mobile, as hurried arrangements were made to meet the emergency. President Mary Dyas of the Florence Military Aid Society drove a wagon to Iuka, Mississippi, and brought casualties back to the society's recently established medical center. Other members assembled at the boat landing "with vehicles of every kind" for carrying men to hospitals and private homes. Future Governor Robert Patton's wife took in several of "the badly shot men in her home," as did many other citizens.[22]

Farther south, in Gainesville, pandemonium took over as scores of broken men poured into a local female college, which had been turned into an emergency hospital. Many of the village's women, accompanied by house slaves, appeared for duty and others took men into their homes. Soon practical nurses of Irish extraction arrived from Mobile and women's organizations throughout the state began sending in supplies. A Eutaw group contributed fresh vegetables and the Selma Military Aid Society donated large amounts of hospital stores, together with an offer to accept any number of men into their "Wayside Homes."[23] Yet, all of this was not sufficient. An experienced hand was needed if the men were to receive proper care.

This need was supplied by Fannie Beers, who responded to the call for volunteers while sojourning with Alabama relatives following a tour of duty at Richmond hospitals. Upon arriving on the scene she found conditions appalling: Here the rooms were crowded with uncomfortable-looking beds, on which lay men whose gangrened wounds gave forth foul odors, which mingled with the terrible effluvia from the mouths of patients ill of scurvy. . . ." Even more shocking was the sight of "a half-dozen women . . . jauntily dressed, airily showing off their patients, and discoursing of their condition and probable chances of life. . . ." Predictably, this experienced matron clashed with these women and, following several conferences with doctors, succeeded in getting the most incompetent ones fired. In short order Fannie reorganized the facilities and was pleased to write that "order and system began to pervade all departments."[24]

While homefront nursing was unquestionably commendable, it was not sufficiently challenging for those Alabamians who wished to do more in behalf of suffering men. As might be expected, there were many so fiercely dedicated that they were willing to abandon the safety of home and family for duty in hospitals nearer the battlefields. Such service appealed to hundreds at first, but few possessed the necessary endurance to last over an appreciable length of time as did Juliet Opie Hopkins, Kate Cumming, Sallie Anne Swope, and the Sisters of Charity. None of these women set out to audition for the role of heroine; that status came by virtue of their tireless labors on the behalf of disabled service men.

Both state and Confederate officials were slow in establishing a medical department, and during the early months they depended on private organizations and individuals to provide hospital facilities. Juliet Opie Hopkins was the first Alabamian to support hospitals for state troops in Virginia. Amazingly, there was nothing in her background to suggest any qualifications or ambitions for such an activity. Her life had been that of a housewife and mother. When the war broke out this Virginia-born matron of forty-two was the wife of Arthur F. Hopkins, a widower twenty-four years her senior, and they lived in comfortable circumstances at Mobile.[25] Opie, as she was generally known, initiated her self-appointed mission in the summer of 1861. With the administrative assistance of her aging husband, three hospitals were founded in Richmond, respectively designated the First, Second, and Third Alabama Hospitals.[26] These were operated as pri-

vate enterprises of the Hopkins family and continued for
several months as self-sufficient institutions until help
came from the state of Alabama.

Mrs. Hopkins did little or no nursing herself, but gave
most of her time to executive duties. According to one of
her nurses, she "kept up a voluminous correspondence,
made in person every purchase for her charges, received
and accounted for hundreds of boxes sent from Alabama
. . . and visited the wards of the hospitals every day," to
make sure that everything ran smoothly.[27] As if this were
not enough, Opie also founded field hospitals at such
places as Culpepper Court House, Yorktown, Bristow
Station, and Monterey.[28]

Obviously indefatigable, she also took it upon herself
to render to the patients of her institutions many personal
services; she wrote letters home for patients, made requests for furloughs, and supplied reading materials to
help pass the long hours of convalescence. A death list of
patients was kept and whenever possible she sent packets
of the deceased patients' hair to the next of kin in Alabama.[29] In fact, no task or sacrifice seemed impossible.
The one supreme test of courage came on July 1, 1862,
when she was twice wounded in the leg while collecting
wounded men on the battlefield at Seven Pines. These in-
juries made an operation necessary, which left her slightly
lame for the rest of her life.[30]

After nearly three months of carrying on alone, assistance came from Alabama on November 9, 1861, when
the legislature created the office of hospital agent, with
the authority to administer state funds earmarked for the
Richmond hospitals. Arthur Hopkins was appointed to
that post and Opie received the title of superintendent of
existing hospitals and also was to have that title over

those that might be established in the future.[31] The following year the Confederate government began phasing out state hospitals by concentrating patients in the two Richmond compounds of Winder and Chimborazo.[32] These changes brought some relief to Mrs. Hopkins but at the same time signaled the beginning of the end of her work in Virginia.

Before the liquidation was effected in 1863, Opie had to deal with a set of dizzying problems that were almost as big and complex as the Confederacy itself. The most pressing was money. However, generous amounts of cash were supplied from the state treasury and by private citizens. Between 1861 and 1863 she acknowledged receiving $73,582.22 from these sources.[33] Moreover, Mrs. Hopkins is credited with contributing her personal fortune, and although it is impossible to fix the exact amount of her donation, one fact is certain—she died in 1890 leaving only a small estate.[34]

For Alabamians everywhere, Opie's exploits became a matter of pure exaltation. Soon she became Alabama's most widely known and respected of the state's hospital workers. According to a spokesman of the Fourth Alabama Regiment, her name was "upon every tongue and prayers . . . daily offered for the friend and benefactor of the sick and wounded soldiers."[35] Congressman Jabez L. M. Curry no doubt pleased her when he wrote expressing his "admiration of, and gratitude for, the sleepless diligence and faithful zeal . . . and tender solicitude with which you have ministered to the . . . sick and suffering soldiers."[36] By far the greatest accolade came from Robert E. Lee, when he said: "You have done more for the South than all the women" of the Confederacy.[37]

Information concerning her activities during the last

years of the war is fragmentary. For a short time in 1864
Opie headed a hospital at Camp Watts near Tuskegee,
but she left that post for a similar position at Montgomery. She remained in the capital until April of 1865, when
she and Mr. Hopkins fled to Newnan, Georgia, to escape
the invading Federal armies.[38] After the war the Hopkins
returned to Mobile and, shortly after the death of her
husband, Opie moved to Washington, D. C., where she
died on March 9, 1890, and was buried with full military
honors in Arlington National Cemetery.[39] Following the
bier was General Joseph E. Johnston, who years before
had dubbed her "The Angel of the South."[40]

On April 11, 1862, Kate Cumming bade her Mobile
family farewell to begin a career as a nurse and matron
with the Army of Tennessee. It was, no doubt, a sad occasion, for Kate was not only leaving home, but she was
entering a service that members of her family considered
altogether unbecoming for refined and cultured ladies. She
was first assigned to duty at a makeshift hospital in Corinth, Mississippi, which had been hastily set up for receiving wounded men from Shiloh. There was absolutely
nothing in this twenty-seven-year-old Scots-born spinster's
life to prepare her to cope with the emergency. It was a
horrible spectacle:

> Gray-haired men—men in the pride of manhood—
> beardless boys—Federals and all, mutilated in every
> imaginable way, lying on the floor, just as they were
> taken from the battlefield; so close together that it
> was impossible to walk without stepping on them.[41]

Without so much as flinching, she began setting up beds,
bathing wounds, and dispensing the medicines prescribed
by the army doctors.

After spending two months of hard nursing in northern Mississippi, she returned home for a well-deserved rest. Meanwhile, the Confederacy granted official status to its nurses. The act of 1862 classified them as chief, assistant, and ward matrons with a monthly salary of forty, thirty-five, and thirty dollars respectively.[42] Kate signed on as a matron and was attached to the mobile hospital system, which followed the Army of Tennessee through several states during the course of the war. In this long trek, she helped in the task of reorganizing hospital facilities time and again, often under the most trying circumstances and at great risk to her life. For example, in 1864, when Federal troops raided the hospital area near Newnan, Georgia, she came under fire, but dauntlessly continued working and afterwards assisted in reestablishing new facilities.[43]

The slaughter of so many young men sometimes made her gray with gloom, but it never shook her resolve. About nursing she would have no nonsense, and she took strong exception to criticism leveled against women hospital workers. Such an attitude was all the more baffling since it appeared to Kate strange for Southern women to consider it a disgrace to do what Florence Nightingale and "aristocratic women of Great Britain have done with honor." Moreover, this patriot looked upon the war as "certainly ours as well as that of the men. We cannot fight, so must take care of those who do."[44]

Kate proved to be a good nurse too, on duty twelve hours some days and on call at night besides. On many occasions she foraged for food and became especially diligent in obtaining much desired buttermilk and fresh eggs for the patients in her wards. When defeat came, Miss Cumming returned home and in 1874 moved to the growing city of Birmingham, where she secured employment as a school teacher. Here she also became active in the Episcopal Church and identified herself with Confederate veterans' organizations. Kate was still unmarried at the time of her death on June 5, 1909.[45]

Indisputably the most colorful nurse from Alabama serving in Virginia was Sallie Swope of Eutaw, Alabama. This inexperienced spinster worked independently of any organization and never held any official position with either state or national governments during four years of selfless service. She just wanted to nurse without fanfare, and for this reason her reputation has been obscured by the more dramatic and well-publicized activities of Opie Hopkins and Kate Cumming. Unfortunately, only fragmentary accounts regarding her career reached Alabama, and even less is known of her origin and life after the war except the bare facts that Miss Swope was born on January 5, 1814, and died on January 31, 1872. She was buried in Tuscaloosa's Greenwood Cemetery and her gravestone carries a simple inscription attesting to her "patriotism and faithfulness in nursing the sick of the Confederate Army."[46]

Contemporary evidence of her arrival in Virginia was first reported by Dr. William H. Sanders in a letter dated August 19, 1861. At that time he wrote that "Miss Swope has not visited our Regt., though we have been looking for her some days."[47] By September, she appeared at Manassas and was judged by Robert Tutwiler, who had seen her at work, to be "very sensible . . . and [she] is an excellent nurse." He expressed disappointment that arrangements could not be worked out for her to stay on with his regiment as a permanent nurse.[48]

Most of Sallie's time was spent in Richmond hospitals

containing Alabama patients. It was here that she attracted the attention of a Eutaw reporter who credited her with "really doing more good than any woman in Richmond. . . ." A whirlwind of activity, she cleaned floors, cooked, nursed, and performed a multitude of other duties demanded by her self-imposed responsibilities. After one battle she personally "secured the bodies of nearly all the fallen . . . from Greene County . . . and had them decently and tenderly interred."[49]

Popularly known as "Miss Sallie" she could be tactless with high-ranking male colleagues, but was gentleness itself with the men in the ranks. One army chaplain affectionately described her as "a character, a Napoleon in her department; with the courage of Andres, she possessed all the energy and independence of 'Stonewall' Jackson." The same observer took special pains in noting that while "the officers hate her; the soldiers adore her." Confederate doctors withered under her cold gaze and dubbed her " 'The Great Eastern' and steered wide of her track. . . ." On one occasion, when a young doctor ordered her out of the hospital for insubordination, she answered with "Pish!" and "swept on in ineffable contempt to the bedside . . . of some sick soldier."[50]

Sallie remained at her post up to the very end. In February of 1865, a friend found her at work among Alabama patients, completely unmindful of the impending dangers of invasion. Concluding that some recognition was due her, this admirer wrote to Alabama's Governor Watts requesting that she be given the rank of matron in the medical department. Such a position, he reasoned, would be at least "hailed by the voices of all the soldiers of Alabama" who had known her work.[51] It is very doubtful if she ever received the title, but it is even more doubtful whether it made any difference to Miss Sallie Swope.

There were many others whose hospital service received only scant contemporary recognition, but few could have been more disinterested in popular acclaim than the Sisters of Charity. Theirs was a nursing order bound by vows to help the sick regardless of rewards or the political and religious beliefs of patients. Yet at times they encountered powerful and fanatic opposition even among the medical profession itself. The fact that most were foreign-born and worked in overwhelmingly Protestant communities made them fit objects for suspicion and hostility. When the six sisters from Mobile took charge of the City Hospital at Warrington, Florida, the men gasped in dismay at the sight of their strange appearance. As one sister tells it, "some covered their heads . . . with blankets and nothing would induce them to uncover . . . for three or four days. . . ." One of the bolder men finally asked if the nuns had been in battles, for if they ever were, he surmised that "the 'Yankees' would be more afraid . . . than any gun the boys could show them. . . ."[52]

Moving with measured efficiency through the unkempt institution, the nuns ordered the building scrubbed, changed beds, and attended to the personal needs of the patients themselves. They also registered strong disapproval at the indifference with which some doctors handled seriously ill cases. Sister Mary Agnes complained to the head physician that "nearly all the fever cases had very serious bed sores and some were fetid with gangrene and two others' clothing had grown in their body." Completely ignored by this official, they went about doing what they could for the unfortunate men. Later on they were ordered back to Mobile, where their services were badly needed for the growing number of war casualties coming into the city.[53]

Even though working conditions in the port city were considerably better, there were emergencies that arose which demanded their immediate attention. When medical supplies ran low at Providence Hospital in 1863, Sister Gabriella volunteered to obtain supplies in northern-occupied New Orleans. After a hard journey of ten days she arrived at the Federal lines, but was refused permission to cross until she took the oath of allegiance. Irate over the delay, the nun reminded the officer in charge that her order was neutral and also that it was engaged in nursing Federal soldiers in the North at that very moment. This explanation completely disarmed him and she was permitted to resume her journey.[54]

The nuns continued on duty during the long siege of Mobile with an air of supreme confidence. As the Federal army closed in around the city in 1865, Sister Gabriella wrote the following dispassionate account of the last days of Confederate Mobile:

> When the Confederates saw that they were obliged to evacuate Mobile their anxiety was, what would they do with their sick and wounded who were not able to be removed from the City. After some deliberation they came to the conclusion to send them to the City Hospital, knowing as they said, that they would not be molested while in the charge of the Sisters of Charity. They sent them all to us. . . . Our hospital was crowded and I hardly knew what to do. . . . Wagon after wagon came and emptied their sick and wounded at our door, the front yard and the street around the hospital were buried with them, it was a cold rainy day, and to leave them there much longer would certainly cause their

death. I had them crowded into every corner of the hospital, and yet there were numbers still lying in the yard. I asked . . . to . . . have the Marine Hospital to put the remainder in and we would take charge of them there. They most gladly gave it to us. I asked . . . Sister Euthelia [Superior of the Female Orphan Asylum] to let me have one of her sisters to go to the Marine Hospital and I sent one of mine over to take charge of them there. We cooked for them here and had to send their meals over every day, this was a great labor, but it did not last long for as soon as the Federals took the City they also took the Marine Hospital for theirs and our sisters left it as their services were no longer required.[55]

root hog or die. . . .

In one way or another every Alabama woman was involved in the Civil War. Like their men, they were substantially united in character and ideals, and in allegiance to the Southern republic. This homogeneity bound women of all classes together in an unusual harmony of purpose and gave them strength and inspiration to engage in work usually performed by men. In the years ahead the myth of feminine helplessness died a hard death as much of the state's economic structure shifted from man power to woman power. The transition was not an easy one for there was much work to be done—much more, in fact, than anyone but the most pessimistic realized. Many were to discover that there was little glamor in facing the staggering problems of running a man's world, missing a meal, and contriving substitutes for the basic necessities of life. As the months unfolded into years, the conflict deepened and life on the home front took on harder lines.

The lives of noncombatants were vexed as well by the growing effectiveness of the blockade, invasion, inflation, and a myriad other maladies of wartime that grew more bewildering and insoluble. It was, for many Alabamians, an end of innocence. However, some successfully adjusted to the role of breadwinner for their families with a minimum of effort, although others sank deeper into the limbo of grinding poverty and were forced to depend on charity for survival.

At first, mistresses left with the part or full-time management of plantations experienced only slight changes in their daily routine. Among the many falling into this category was Ella Storrs Christian of near Uniontown, who welcomed the additional responsibilities and noted that "nothing of moment broke the smooth current of home life from day to day, though we were always unhappy and troubled about the army." Aside from that the future looked bright and her day dreams were filled with plans for building "a handsome house, on a hill" after the war.[1] She, however, confessed to being kept very busy feeding and clothing the slaves, and directing them in their daily planting chores. The days were also taken up with housekeeping and nursing sick servants, and when manufactured articles gave out, she lamented the difficulties of having to search the community for necessary replacement. All of this was clearly enough to keep any mistress busy around the clock, but the schedule continued until 1865, when invasion put an end to her tenure.

Experiencing similar responsibilities was Martha Jane Crossley of Perote, who operated every facet of plantation management while her brothers fought in the war. In addition to supervising the planting activities, she cultivated a home garden of vegetables, canned fruits from the orchard, and tended her flower garden of roses and japonicas. A deeply religious woman, Martha had evening sessions of Bible reading for her slaves and once recorded in her diary that "the soul of a poor humble slave influenced to seek salvation by . . . precept and example will shine as bright in our starry crown as that of a king."

When the supply of salt ran low, this mistress sent "Bud Jim," the slave overseer, to Florida's gulf coast to make some from sea water. Later on she stationed two slaves on the coast to provide a steady supply, but this venture ended in November, 1862, when Union gunboats destroyed the Crossley salt-making apparatus. On learning of the disaster, she was first concerned for the welfare of the slaves and dropped to her knees to pray for their safety.[2]

For members of the plantation set everywhere, the war brought on a series of challenges undreamed of during the piping days of peace. Many of those who had enjoyed a languid existence as first lady of the manor were suddenly forced into the command of family estates while their men served in the army or entered government service. Saddled with such a burden was Mrs. C. C. Clay, Sr., of Madison County; even though Alabama's ex-first lady was past sixty she proved herself to be an astute planter. From the first she produced more food crops than cotton, and in reporting the innovation to her son in the Confederate Senate, she urged him to use his influence in making this change a mandatory requirement for all Southern planters. At the same time she resolved to remain on duty "even if the Yankees" invaded north Alabama.[3]

The enemy did come, first on April 11, 1862, and many other times during the war. Her aging husband was imprisoned, but shortly was released on condition that he remain at home. During the first occupation, the Clays suffered heavy losses in property, but when the Confederates returned in August of 1862, Mrs. Clay again resumed complete control of the family holdings. This time her task was made harder, for the presence of the Yankees had seriously curtailed production at the height of the

growing season and the slaves had become badly demoralized. Some had run away and others refused to work. In
an attempt to restore discipline she tried moral suasion,
but was only partially successful.

"The negroes," she wrote to her son, "are ignorant &
grasping, as we are, for a happier future. I have a hard
time with ours, for they do as they like. I try 'moral suasion' to get them to do their duty. It sometimes succeeds."
A year later she wrote that "the negroes are worse than
free, they say they *are* free. We cannot expect any authority. I beg ours to do what little is done." Susanna Clay
was constantly beset with labor problems and never completely regained mastery over the slave work force. By
1865 she sorrowfully informed her son that:

> We have lost all, almost. . . . Your father and myself
> have the wing of the house. We stay in it as the negroes
> left long since. Our house has been occupied the greater
> time. I rented the upper rooms to people who turned
> out to be actors. They have paid part and I hope to get
> the balance. . . . Our beautiful town is desolated. Our
> church injured . . . the Methodist Church was burned;
> the small *Episcopal Church* is occupied by them.[4]

Maintaining firm control over house slaves became a
vexing problem for Mrs. W. D. Chadick, the wife of a
Confederate army chaplain and neighbor of the Clay
family. Her wartime diary abounds in statements attesting
to what she considered slave rascality and slothfulness
while Union forces occupied Huntsville. She recorded the
deepest disappointment when several favorite servants
left her to work for the wives of United States officers.
The façade of loyalty was torn away at last and she wrote
that "such is a foretaste of what we will have to go

through with when the rebellion is quashed and the wonderful 'Yankee Nation' gets possession of 'Niggerdom'."
In 1864 when the last slave domestic announced her intention of following a military unit North, Mrs. Chadick
tried earnestly to change her mind. Accordingly, the white
woman wrote of the encounter:

> I . . . spoke to Corinna, and asked her where and why
> she was going. She was first inclined to be impudent and
> impolite, but when I talked kindly to her, she changed
> her tone and said . . . if things had not gone so far,
> she would not go. I told her that I did not ask her to
> stay, but if she was ever in want or needed a home, she
> could come back, and that she would be kindly treated.
> She commenced crying and the Yankees hurried her off.[5]

It is hardly surprising that some failed at plantation
management. Under normal conditions it was no easy job
and, indeed, during the antebellum period many men possessing years of experience had done no better with this
most demanding enterprise. As might be expected, there
were women living in the safe areas of Alabama who
found it impossible to carry on alone and asked to be re-
lieved of the responsibilities. For example, in 1861 Mary
Fitzpatrick admitted that she could not manage the slaves
and pleaded with her husband to come home "right
away."[6]

There were many others so desperate that they peti-
tioned state officials for relief. Such was the case of Jane
Brasfield of Greene County when she wrote Governor
Shorter to use his influence with President Davis in getting
her son returned from the army so that he could take over
the family plantation. "The negroes . . . are now pretty
much at the mercy of their own will," she explained, and

continued, "one man has already run away with the intention of going to the Yankee army and . . . doubtlessly he will inspire others to do the same." The distraught woman went on to say that her son was the only person capable of disciplining the slaves and for that reason he should be sent home immediately.[7]

Still another mistress, living near Summerfield, requested an exemption for her overseer on the grounds that her "place needs a man to overlook things" chiefly because ill health prevented her from adequately managing a 920-acre plantation containing over fifty slaves. She went on to remind the governor to "think of the situation your wife would be in were she placed as I am." A Mrs. A. S. McCain pleaded the same circumstances in writing for an exemption for her son. She also argued that since other members of her family were already in the army one exemption could not possibly hurt the Confederate cause.[8]

Among the most persistent problems confronting Alabama women was that of obtaining the basic necessities of life. As they were cut off from outside sources by the blockade, and all available transportation facilities were preempted for military purposes, all household heads were forced to practice a self-sufficient economy similar to that of the pioneer period. Improvisation became a way of life as homefront civilians found ways of contriving substitutes out of the materials at hand. Home garden plots were enlarged and cultivated with great care for those crops that could be processed into sugar, tea, coffee, and other scarce commodities. Many a housewife shared recipes with neighbors for making cakes out of watermelon rind preserves, tea from parched strawberry leaves, and coffee from roasted Irish or sweet potato peelings. The skins of slaughtered livestock were a prime source for shoe leather, and were often dyed with a mixture of soot and oil.

Ella Storrs Christian was typical of those who utilized a wide range of raw materials found on her Perry County plantation. She created hand and face lotion from mutton suet and added the juices of honeysuckle, rose, or jasmine blossoms to make that cosmetic more esthetically acceptable. One of the scarcest commodities was candles, and she frequently complained of the difficulty of getting the soft beeswax to remain erect, but finally hit upon the solution of winding heavily coated wicks around corn cobs.[9]

Almost nothing was overlooked in the quest for medical substitutes after patented remedies were exhausted. Forest and fields were explored for herbs known to possess curative powers, and long-neglected recipes were revived in the compounding of necessary medicines. Castor oil was extracted from the plants that grew in profusion on the Barbour County plantation where Parthenia Hague was employed as a teacher. She also told how opium was derived from home-grown poppies, and attested to the fact that it was "not unexcelled by that of the imported article in its effects."[10] Mary L. Fleming of Dale County told in her postwar reminiscences of the unpleasant experience of having to take spring tonics made from dogwood and cherry tree barks. Although this little rebel was less than enthusiastic over the medicines, she did enjoy herself making substitute drinking glasses from old bottles, and milk pails from the ends of cedar logs.[11]

As was true of women everywhere, Alabamians evinced a keen interest in their personal wardrobes and despite shortages proved especially ingenious in producing a Confederate vogue of makeshift fashions. Prewar wearing apparel was usually reserved for special occasions; when necessary it was meticulously mended or altered to keep abreast of the changes in the styles of the day. Fashion-conscious women converted draperies, rugs, bedding, and remnant items stored in old trunks into dresses and other wearing apparel. Gradually homespun, that mainstay material of the poor, came to dominate the fashion scene and women of all segments of society proudly wore the coarse material. Hats were woven out of palmetto, straw, and vines, and the press gallantly went all out in praising those women who were cheerfully wearing the makeshift garments. One contemporary observer boldly gave his critique of a well-dressed Confederate lady "fitted in homespun wearing a palmetto hat as the loveliest sight that a true Southern born man may behold."[12]

On the other hand, no amount of flattery could take the place of new and stylish outfits, and shortly before the war's end the makeshift existence became a bore for even the most patriotic Confederates. Early in 1865 Kate Cumming, no pace setter in style, acknowledged that "there is no necessity of . . . discussing war or politics . . . as we have an all-absorbing topic in the matter of dress and 'something to eat.' " "How do you manage to live?" or "What have you to wear?" became common conversation openers with women everywhere. She also reported that her Mobile friends never succumbed to the propaganda extolling the charms of homespun dresses. Most had always preferred one good calico to three homespun frocks. In fact, Kate herself lamented the high prices charged for every necessity of life and predicted that in th future "we will be charged for the light of Heaven and the air we breathe."[13]

As the cost of living rose scores of women had to earn a living outside the home. A few found employment in the limited number of war industries of the state, but the paucity of records makes it impossible to determine the total number involved or the pay scale of female laborers. Nevertheless, in 1862 one newspaper correspondent reported seeing eighty girls rolling cartridges and working at "gun manufactory" in a primitive munitions plant located near Gainesville.[14] There were better employment opportunities at the munition center of Selma and even though men were preferred Emily Ferguson reminisced in later years that "many young ladies" worked in several arsenals for pay.[15] Indigent women and children were also employed in the textile industry, but hundreds lost their jobs when the mills were destroyed during an invasion. The burning of a Bibb County cotton factory in 1865 struck one observer as "a most unfortunate affair" because it resulted in the loss of livelihood for many of "the poorer classes of women and children" from Bibb and surrounding counties.[16]

Home industries came into being as enterprising women supplemented family incomes from the sale of preserved fruit, plain and fancy sewing, and a great variety of other hand-crafted items. They also marketed soap and cured meats when supplies were available, but one of the most lucrative enterprises was nitre-making. The government offered 75¢ per pound and made frequent appeals in newspapers for this essential element in the production of gunpowder. "Every old lady," ran an advertisement in 1862, "that knows how to have an ash hopper put up can make it" from soils in caves, stables, and other high nitrogen content soils.[17] Margaret Rogers of Orrville was given credit for supplying Selma factories with "the first specimen of domestic manufactured nitre."[18] Others followed suit, but such sources soon proved inadequate.

By 1863 nitre was being derived from human urine and Jonathan Haralson, the agent in charge of the Selma Nitre and Mining Bureau, requested that the women of the city contribute the contents of their chamber pots. No remuneration was offered, but in order to avoid embarrassment to the donors, government wagons were assigned to collect the containers during the early morning hours.[19] This unconventional situation created an entertaining furor among Selma men and seeing the wagons make their appointed rounds stirred Thomas B. Wetmore to soaring heights of satirical doggerel. The following is one of the three stanzas lampooning the project:

> Jno. Haralson! Jno. Haralson!
> Where did you get that notion
> Of sending barrels around our Streets
> To fill them with that lotion?
> We thought the women did enough
> At sewing shirts and kissing:
> But you have put the lovely dears
> to Patriotic P — — — — — g.[20]

Haralson could not let such chiding pass unchallenged and accordingly responded with two verses, of which the second ran:

> Women will stoop to conquer
> And keep their virtue pure.
> It is no harm to kill a beast
> With Chamber lye, I'm sure.
> But powder we are bound to have,
> And this we've sworn before

That if the needful thing is scarce
They'll press it, and 'Wetmore.'

In the struggle for survival those who had known better days took in boarders and engaged in small business enterprises. Even Mrs. Basil Manly, the wife of the former president of the University of Alabama, rented rooms and furnished meals to a select clientele.[21] Quick lunches were sold from "little huckster stands" located on street corners or at depots. One Montgomery woman specialized in serving hard-boiled eggs, bread, and fried fish which one soldier-customer described "as hot and done to a crisp—actually frying in my mouth," but despite the pyrotechnics he pronounced it "good, I tell you."[22] Others sold trinkets and notions of every conceivable variety, but the most popular were the little pastry stands stocked with cookies, breads, and pies. However, some business women stinted on the ingredients and according to a customer of a LaGrange, Alabama, peddler, her sweet potato pies were "tasteless in the extreme."[23]

The impact of war on Alabama's infant public education system was immediately felt in the drastic cut in funds and the loss of male teachers to the draft. A similar situation plagued private institutions and in many communities schools closed for the duration of the war and others barely managed to survive with a staff of poorly paid female instructors. The antebellum stigma against women in education vanished everywhere as necessity forced many a proud and formerly affluent woman into earning a living in the classroom. Almost no one was rejected and even inexperienced teenage girls were eagerly accepted, as is illustrated in the case of one identified only as Fannie when she was hired to teach at a Pine Level school. One of Fannie's relatives, who had previously taken a dim view of women teachers, now considered teaching as "fine employment for our Confederate girls in the absence of all our gentlemen teachers." Besides, "little Fannie" had the reputation of being "so good everybody loves her, and so sweet and dignified that she is fully competent to teach though she is only sixteen."[24]

Every wartime teacher worked under great handicaps, not the least of which was the serious shortages in such instructional materials as pencils, paper, ink, and textbooks. Typical of this state of affairs was rural Dale County, where Mary L. Fleming described her experience in wartime schools. According to her postwar memoirs, she attended institutions at Pleasant Hill and Westfield, both of which were located several miles from her farm home. Academic terms ran four months in the winter and two in the summer. Women substituted for men most of the time, but from time to time discharged soldiers with little or no training acted as teachers.

Textbooks consisted of prewar grammars, readers, and spellers, which were handled with great care since it was impossible to obtain new supplies. If a section of the lesson was missing from one pupil's book, he studied with another until he reached that part where the text began again in his book. Brothers and sisters often had to use the same text, switching around when they were not in the same class. Discipline was hard and Mary recorded receiving a severe whipping for spilling milk on the floor. Yet, like all youngsters, they managed to have good times together. The little girls often spent nights with their schoolmates and played such games as blind man's bluff until "the old folks stopped us and sent us to bed. . . ."[25]

Salaries were never munificent and varied widely from

place to place. Some rebel schoolmarms received only room and board from parents, together with a small stipend of cash ranging from three to ten dollars a month. Most, however, were dedicated souls and remained on the job even during periods of invasion and occupation. A few even expressed the intention of remaining in the profession after the war, even though their first impressions of teaching amounted to a frightening experience. At the end of her first week, Nannie Rayburn of Oakland wrote a friend setting forth an agonizing reappraisal of herself: "Oh! the responsibility, it makes my very spirit tremble, when I think of it. To think I am giving bent to mortal minds, stamping character for eternity." "Even today," she continued, "I have seen the little children aping me, assuming my every action," and closed with a plea for prayers so that "I may be guided by unerring wisdom to set examples worthy of being followed."[26]

Institutions of higher education for women, although as limited in instructional materials as those of the elementary level, continued to receive students. Among those that remained open throughout the war were Judson in Marion, two women's colleges at Tuskegee, and scores of private academies located outside the war zones of the state. In fact, at the beginning of the war the Gainesville Female College boasted that its standards were "as good as if there was not a war in the land." However, the headmistress confessed that a shortage of books existed, but she surmised that such inconveniences would be easily remedied by "the diligence in studying the few we have here."[27] In less than a year this so-called college was commandeered as a Confederate hospital, but so were many other educational institutions as the war came closer to Alabama.

Although hardly anyone was immune from economic difficulties, the hardest hit were the families of yeoman farmers and poor whites. For the women of this class the war became a deepening nightmare of survival under the most trying circumstances. They owned no plantations or slaves for support, and they were, in the main, poorly educated farmers' wives who had labored along with their husbands in eking out a marginal livelihood from small farming operations located in the pine barrens and mountainous sections of the state. When their men went into the army, many of them were doomed to a life of lonely and matriarchal penury.

Almost from the beginning of the war women could be seen plowing in the fields, marketing crops, and engaging in other farming chores. While stationed near Mobile in 1862, Edward H. Moren was unprepared for such a sight and wrote his wife how shocked he was to realize that "the women . . . have to plow and sow, reap and live on the principle of 'root hog or die.' "[28] Moren failed to mention that the principal cause of women's having to work so hard could be partially laid at the door of the Confederate conscription acts. They had to work hard or starve. In some of the "white counties" draft quotas worked great hardships upon the female population. For example, in 1862 one concerned citizen of Shelby County estimated that within two weeks after one draft call "there will be three hundred females at the handle of the plow," and although he was convinced that "they are patriotic ladies & will stand between the handles . . . with great bravery" he wanted to apprise the governor of the fact that Shelby could not sustain any further drain on its manpower.[29]

Hunger and pain became facts of everyday life for

those physically unable to work in the fields. Indeed, many hundreds of poor soldiers' families who were left manless lived close to starvation in practically every section of the state. A poor woman from Coffee County, for example, reported knowing several "soldiers wives . . . living on bread alone and entirely without salt" and many others who had to subsist on thirty pounds of meat and twelve bushels of corn each as a year's rations.[30] Conditions became so unbearable to one Russell County woman that she and her children fled to relatives in Georgia, but finding no relief there, she implored the governor for help to prevent her family from starving.[31] Like plantation mistresses many were unable to carry on alone and sought official intercession to alleviate conditions. Emily Hewlett was one of scores who wrote the governor begging that her son be released from the army so that he might resume management of her Walker County farm.[32] The poorly educated Sarah Driggers of Coffee County asked that the chief executive have "merci and cumpasion on a pore disconsolat mother and have my Dear Son Sent hom" because "I am a pore woman and have no one to assis me on earth."[33]

Private agonies gradually became general agonies and others combined to petition state authorities for an exemption of those men deemed essential to the survival of underdeveloped communities. A group from County Line, Alabama, asked the governor to excuse W. A. Steed from military service not only because he made shoes for the villagers, taught school, marketed farm products, but also because he constituted their only source of protection against outlaws who might have seized "what little we have for our *helpless children*."[34] The same fate was predicted for the Pine Grove community in Coosa County if their only male protector was drafted into the army.[35]

Impressment of slaves for military purposes also added to the misery of poor families dependent on neighboring plantations for food and other supplies. After an especially heavy quota was taken from Talladega County in 1864, a group of angry citizens registered a vigorous protest with the governor and pointed out that there were 3,997 destitute persons wholly dependent "for subsistence upon the slave labor in the valley," as were many others who had come into their community from Coosa, Tallapoosa, Randolph, and parts of Calhoun counties. In their opinion any further requisitions would be "suicide for the government to take our labor . . . now when we are planting crops and doing all we can to raise provisions."[36] An even more critical situation existed in Randolph County, where 33½% of the slaves had been whisked away. Here 8,000 were on relief and any future drain on manpower might result in the repetition of civil disturbances such as the one that occurred in 1863. This was a women-led food riot "in which Government wheat and corn had been seized to prevent starvation of themselves and families. Where it will end, unless relief is afforded, we cannot tell."[37]

The women's battle for survival was further intensified as war profiteers, left to their own self-seeking devices, charged exorbitant prices for essential food and clothing supplies. Nearly every community was plagued by these merchants, farmers, and planters who first doubled, then tripled the cost of such Southern staples as bacon, cornmeal, and molasses. While there were, to be sure, a fortunate few who could afford the steep prices, there were thousands of the state's poor reduced to destitution by homegrown speculators. Many articulate women deplored

this nefarious practice and frequently raised complaints in
the press against every form of profiteering. A "Country
Woman" of Dallas County blamed all the woes besetting
"the widows and wives of soldiers squarely on the shoul-
ders of speculators and extortioners."[38] Hastening to
agree was a fellow citizen signing herself as "Z," but she
enlarged the indictment and blamed government officials
for not imposing strict price controls. In strengthening her
case for immediate action, "Z" called attention to the
plight of hundreds of poor women of her acquaintance
"who are now without sugar . . . molasses . . . coffee,
eggs, and . . . meat." Some, indeed, were having to feed
their children corn bread and water as "their only food"[39]

Hardly a week passed without a contumelious attack on
speculators, and the governor's office was bombarded with
pleas for help. A report came from Marshall County in
July, 1862, that corn was selling at $1.25 per bushel and
that many women and children were literally crying for
bread. The following year the governor was asked to stop
Walker County "misers" from buying all the potatoes in
the area for "the purpose of distilling them into ardent
spirits" while soldiers' families were in desperate need of
food.[40] Early in 1864 a Washington County sexagenarian
named J. A. Sullivan wrote that he knew of one soldier's
wife who had to pick "berrys to keep from starving" and
there were many others forced into "boiling potatoe vines
to subsist on . . ." while the "rich had their Board spred
with dainties. . . ." This class-conscious gentleman claimed
to possess evidence that certain planters in his neighborhood were not only charging unreasonable prices for food
but some were actually demanding "20 to 25 dolar a pair
for shoes. . . ."[41]

As economic conditions grew steadily worse, the specter

of civil strife raised its head in several Alabama communities. Because of inability to cope with speculation, inflation, and scarcities, "bread riots", as already noted, occurred in Randolph County, but the most violent broke out in Mobile in April and September of 1863. In the latter month a rootless mob of women carrying placards emblazoned with "Bread or Blood" surged into the streets looting stores and physically assaulting merchants who had been known to charge exorbitant prices. Armed with pitchforks and kitchen utensils, they had their own way for the better part of a day, and when the city constabulary failed to restore order the Seventeenth Alabama Regiment was called in. However, when the men discovered the rioters to be "starving wives, mothers, sisters, and daughters" of service men, they returned to their barracks without firing a shot. Peace was restored only after city officials promised to do their best in getting food prices reduced and most returned home "promise crammed," but not before vocally registering determination to get relief or return the following day and "burn the whole city."[42]

Early in the war, the tragic condition of thousands of poor families had aroused the state government into action and between 1861 and 1865 the legislature released $11,800,000[43] of public funds for the relief of 43,299 families or 169,036 individuals.[44] In addition, measures were passed granting special dispensations for soldiers' families, such as exempting widows of deceased volunteers from paying taxes on property valued up to $500 and furnishing medicines free of charge to indigent families of service men.[45] Not to be overlooked was the state's distribution of free cotton and wool cards along with textiles to those needy persons engaged in manufacturing clothing for their families.[46] County governing bodies were also authorized to levy special taxes and issue securities in raising funds for poor relief. In most of the wealthy communities the office of "special agent" was created to administer the procuring and distribution of food stuffs to the needy at cost or as outright gifts. While official and local charities accounted for much relief for the suffering, it was far from adequate in coping with the situation and the problem was still present when Alabama fell to Union forces in 1865.

In enemy-occupied areas bare subsistence became just as difficult, but aid soon came from Federal officials. The records abound in instances of charity rendered by army officers and enlisted men who were moved by the pitiful conditions of destitute women living in the Tennessee Valley. Such was the case with General M. G. Thomas when he ordered that a Mrs. Austin and a Miss Elizabeth Green of Bridgeport be given "sufficient supplies to keep them from starving."[47] Many others swallowed their pride in the urge for survival, as did Mrs. W. D. Chadick, and during the times Huntsville came under occupation she frequently drew rations from Federal commissaries. On October 4, 1864, for example, she received several months of supplies, consisting of "four pounds of sugar, two and a half pounds of coffee, 22 pounds of bacon, and a half box of crackers."[48] This Confederate chaplain's wife deeply regretted having to depend on the enemy's largess, but at no time did she return any of the dole. Although she never said so in her diary, there is the nuance of suspicion that she considered herself lucky and far better off than her sister Confederates in unoccupied Alabama.

8

fresh, frank, fun-loving girls

As was the case throughout Dixie, the War for Southern Independence also afforded Alabama women countless opportunities for the pursuit of pleasure. Except for those holding extreme puritanical views, most feminine noncombatants could see no harm in enjoying themselves at dances, at parties, and in participating in a multitude of other public and private diversions common to nineteenth-century society. After all, they were contributing much of their time and energy in behalf of the war effort and deserved the chance to get some fun out of life. If an explanation for levity became necessary, there was always the handy excuse of entertaining for the purpose of making Southern warriors happy or to raise money for this or that charitable project.

More often than not, high-spirited young women could not have cared less about any charges of frivolity. They blithely concentrated much of their attention on having a good time whenever possible and, at least for the moment, the actualities of war receded into the background. The war also offered affluent hedonists unlimited opportunities to revel as never before; many of this group gamboled about in search of fun with great gusto and unprecedented sophistication. Others, somewhat more inhibited, discov-

148

ered discreet ways of evading custom and convention without seriously offending prudish parents and neighbors.

Public displays of affection soon became commonplace and young men and women alike grew bolder as the war quickened the pace of courtship practices. Almost everywhere couples could be seen promenading arm in arm, exchanging admiring glances, and sometimes cuddling or slyly kissing one another. Railroad stations became the setting where many a young lover warmly embraced her fiancé on leavetaking and as a greeting to those returning from battle fronts. Romantic couples were likely to be seen any place or at any time of day. On a train trip to Alabama in 1863, Mary Chesnut's attention was directed by her slave maid to a couple who were "irrepressibly kissing and lolling against each other." The South Carolina senator's wife had often witnessed such scenes before, but this time she was mildly surprised at the man's insistence that his companion "brush his cheek with those beautiful eyelashes of hers."[1]

The more discriminating couples sought less conspicuous places and it was reported that proper Montgomerians engaged in much "love making . . . on horseback" during long rides in the countryside. One young woman, who had accepted a proposal of marriage while mounted on a restless steed, was asked by friends as to how it was possible to seal the bargain with a kiss under the circumstances. She gave the evasive answer that they did not, but that they quoted the poetry of "Byron a good deal."[2] Members of the older set of Montgomery enjoyed embracing one another at social gatherings. It would seem that kissing became a common practice at home dances and parties, judging from the testimony given by those who kept records of such events. During one Christmas season

Sarah Follansbee tells of attending a series of dinner parties; at one of which she was delighted to be the recipient of a veritable marathon of kisses from every married man present. The usually staid Baptist-bred spinster made no objections and recorded that she and the merrymakers danced past midnight, after which all enjoyed a hearty Yuletide feast.[3]

The ancient art of coquetry seemed in no way to have diminished on account of the war but was, if anything, intensified as rebel girls employed their own special techniques in attracting soldier-suitors who were stationed in Alabama. Well-bred young ladies and those not so fortunate in social background both knew full well the drawing power of a sly wink, the contrived blush, the demure smile, and countless other little gestures that were designed to show amicable intentions. Undeniably, most males were inclined to respond in kind and nature took its inevitable course. At least University of Alabama Cadet Frank E. Bestor found much pleasure in flirting with Tuscaloosa girls whom he saw on the streets and whom he approvingly accused of being "tolerable fast." More especially, he enjoyed the presence of the coquettes who gathered to watch retreat parades every afternoon on the campus, mainly because they formed a veritable pool of potential dates for the evening.[4]

Harmless flirtations provided amusement and no doubt mutual satisfaction for a select few aristocratic married women who moved in that society populated by high-ranking army officers in Richmond. A typical case was that of Celeste Clay who candidly wrote how pleasant it was to conduct "a nice little flirtation" with General Howell Cobb, from whom she extracted the promise to care for her in case her husband "falls in action."[5]

As was to be expected, objections arose when flirting got out of hand or posed threats to the canons of Victorian deportment. From time to time parents or guardians took a hand in disciplining brazen daughters, but some objections came from country girls unable to compete with the charms of visiting city relatives and friends. When the sophisticated Mary Russell of Mobile went to Tompkinsville, Alabama, in 1861 for a visit, she created quite a stir among the villagers, but more especially among the young ladies, of whom she wrote that they were "not the best pleased in the world to see me for I took some of their beaux . . . before and they are a little afraid of me." She continued, "The old ladies, think it high time I was thinking about 'seeking religion' . . . and there is to be a protracted meeting here . . . then I know they will try to get me to the 'Mourners bench,' if they can get me to church." Miss Russell thought of going just for the sheer fun of seeing the congregation "shout when they got religion" and also to flirt with the handsome men.[6]

Some threw propriety to the winds and when such conduct resulted in scandal, they were condemned as either immoral creatures or unfortunate victims of that moral lassitude engendered by the war. In some communities the paucity of men forced fun-loving mature women to seek the company of teen-age males. "You may think it exaggeration," wrote Thomas B. Hall to a kinsman in the army, "when I tell you that little boys not over thirteen or fourteen . . . are flying around grown young ladies in Montgomery," and he went on to express pity for such women who so desperately needed some one to admire them, but failed to accord the same feelings for the boys in question.[7]

Clergymen, too, came in for criticism primarily because

their military exemption made them the only men around
for lonesome women to admire and pursue as fit companions. Many were accused of committing all sorts of
mischief, as in the case of one young minister of Greensboro of whom it was said that he had "destroyed his use-
fulness . . . by getting into a terrible love scrape" with a
girl of his congregation. The affair supplied many de-
licious hours of gossip and one wag authoritatively predicted that "the matter will likely come to trouble."[8] Talk
of extramarital relations with ministers was whispered to
Mary Chesnut while she lived in Montgomery in 1861.
She was once told that a companion of hers was having
an illicit affair with a local preacher who, it seemed, first
prayed with the object of his affection and subsequently
stayed with her. A short time later Mrs. Chesnut learned
that her informant was no better and had given birth to
a baby "too soon after her marriage."[9]

The Civil War was largely responsible for an increase
in the number of marriages as thousands of engaged couples rushed to the altar before the man left for the service
or while he was at home on furlough. Amusement-starved
women everywhere flocked to both simple and elaborate
weddings, where they could gain a little respite from the
sad events of wartime existence by mingling with friends,
shedding a few tears of joy, and catching up on the latest
gossip. Some, indeed, seemed to have made a career of
attending weddings, as did Mary Mitchell Williamson of
Autauga County, who went to great lengths to indulge in
her favorite form of entertainment. To her there was no
such thing as an unhappy wedding. All of the more than
a dozen at which she was a guest during 1862 proved
memorable affairs and she invariably wrote "pleasant,
pleasant" in her diary after attending each one.[10]

The Clay women of Huntsville were frequently seen at weddings and receptions of locally prominent families when the north Alabama town was free of Yankee occupation. In 1862 Mary Clay rhapsodized eloquently in describing the "sumptuous tea" following the Longanan marriage. "I sat in the drawing room," she wrote Virginia, "and saw all the pretty girls and the handsome supper table brilliantly lighted with kerosene oil and parafin candles. . . . There were no meats," she regretfully noted, "but ice cream, strawberries, Charlotte ruses, fruit cakes, sponge gold and silver cakes, and everything in abundance."[11]

There were brilliant weddings to attend, like that of Eliza Sims, the daughter of J. Marion Sims, to Dr. J. T. Pratt, a Confederate army surgeon. Held in Paris, France, on March 17, 1864, it was reported to be "a Confederate wedding in all its surroundings." The ceremony took place at the bride's home, where the parlors were decorated in Confederate colors, and it was attended by "numerous Confederate naval officers in their gray uniforms." In point of fact, everything was in gray except the bride, who wore the traditional white and carried a bouquet decorated with tiny Confederate flags. Among the civil dignitaries present was John Slidell, "the official representative of the Confederacy to meet the requirements of the French law touching the legality of the marriage" in France. After a "Confederate reception" the couple departed for an American honeymoon—ostensibly to the Confederate States of America.[12]

Quite expectedly, there was some parents who objected to war marriages. Numerous instances are recorded in private records attesting to the impropriety of certain unions during the war on account of incompatability or the lack of pecuniary means for supporting the brides. One of these was registered by Dr. Basil Manly of Tuscaloosa, who performed his son's nuptial ceremony with grave misgivings because he disapproved of the bride. In harsh words, which he confided to his diary, Manly wrote that he was "never satisfied of the propriety of the union . . . under any circumstances, especially since I have seen in her, as a pupil, the want of an earnest and thoughtful mind. . . ." Moreover, he knew that his son would be unable to support a wife on a soldier's pay and, what was worse, "we are ignorant whether she has a dime . . . in her own right . . . on which she may rely for support."[13]

Although the war brought about a reduction of social activities almost everywhere in Alabama, the sharpest decline took place in villages and isolated rural areas. It was here that many women had to experience the most monotonous hours of their lives. Deprived of male companionship, and because of the almost complete lack of amusement, most of them were compelled to find surcease from boredom in reading, church work, and visits with the neighbors. The more resourceful did find social outlets in aid societies or in preparing food specialties for exhibit at county fairs, but the majority spent their leisure time sitting on their front porches, eagerly anticipating an unexpected visitor or pining after their menfolk.

In the occupied areas entertainment opportunities were generally reduced to those affairs given by the enemy. But most Alabama women boycotted Yankee socials and devised ways of amusing themselves in the company of their fellow Confederates. Mrs. W. D. Chadick tells of making frequent house calls on Southern friends in Huntsville and how much she and her children enjoyed each others' company at the family vacation cottage in nearby Monte Sano.

The Chadicks also found much pleasure in Christmas celebrations and other holiday seasons. On one occasion she sent two friends a spurious "official document" that called for the eviction of their property for military personnel. After deriving "some fun" from the consternation that ensued, she admitted that it was only an April Fool's joke.[14]

On the other hand, the war did furnish urban women with better opportunities for social outlets in the form of dances, theatricals, and parties—most of which were designed to raise funds for worthwhile causes. In every city and in most county-seat towns, social leaders took turns sponsoring musical concerts featuring local talent. In 1861 a large audience of Montgomerians attended a musical performance given by four young girls seated at two pianos. As an added attraction a local band played such stirring songs as the "Southern Marseillaise" and other popular selections of the day. According to a newspaper account the entire programs was judged to be "a magnificent way" of obtaining money for the Soldiers' Fund.[15]

Shortly afterwards, the manager of Montgomery's Estelle Hall reported that a full house was present on the evening of September 23, 1861, to see the premier showing of "the Ponoption—a large oil painting on rolls depicting the stirring Revolution in which we are engaged." Musical accompaniment was supplied by Fannie Fitz, who, it was said, "executed patriotic selections with silver bells in the most elegant style."[16] This attraction remained on the marquee for several weeks and the proceeds were donated to the Ladies' Aid Association.

Large crowds of men and women also paid admission to hear concerts staged by female college students at commencement exercises. Quite typical of this kind of enter-

tainment was a performance sponsored by the seniors of
the Tuscaloosa Female College in August of 1861. The
finale brought down the house in "spontaneous applause"
as the graduates sang "Dixie" while dressed in costumes
bearing the coats of arms of the various Confederate
States.[17]

Wartime theatricals and professional lecturers supplied
much entertainment for many city women and almost
everything was offered, ranging from grand opera, com-
edies, poetry readings, and patriotic speeches to classical
dances, performed, in the main, by amateur talent. Occasionally small towns were visited by traveling shows or
individual artists of the performing arts. In early 1861
"Blind Tom," the negro mimic and pianist, thrilled Gainesville audiences with his rendition of the "Rain Drop
Waltz" and other popular compositions.[18] Whenever the
war permitted, parties, picnics, and barbecues abounded
in every section, but the all-time favorite of Alabamians
everywhere was tableaux vivants. These performances,
too, were usually staged for raising money to help a particular cause. Such was the purpose of one held in Selma in
1861, which boasted a cast of "large numbers of the
beauty and fashion" of the Black Belt Town. The price of
admission was in kind, and large amounts of socks, flannel
and wool underclothing, and various food items were deposited at the box office.[19]

With very few exceptions these attractions consisted of
young girls portraying living statues featuring a patriotic
scene. For instance, on December 23, 1861, a Mobile
tableau depicted a wounded Confederate soldier being ad-
ministered treatment by a bevy of attractively dressed
young women. Despite their efforts the hero died, but not
before conveying the idea that Alabama women were ever

ready "to touch water to his parching lips and endeavoring with tender hands to staunch his bloody wound."[20] Regardless of quality and sameness of themes, tableaux dramas paid handsome dividends and monies derived from these productions poured into the governor's office during the war years. For example, in 1862 a young women's group in Notasulga sent in $68 representing the net proceeds of a tableau, which amount they requested be used toward helping buy hospital supplies.[21] Others earmarked the funds for other charities. A Eutaw group sent in $82 to be used toward helping the families of "needy Alabama soldiers."[22]

Rivaling tableaux in profit and popularity were lotteries that offered a great variety of prizes ranging from livestock to cotton bales, and many women failed to see any harm in sponsoring such projects so long as the proceeds went to some charitable organization. During the first year the "raffle craze" took on epidemic proportions and, in turn, brought about serious criticism from ministers and the press. Typical of dozens of editorials against lotteries was one published at Opelika, in which such activity was condemned not only because it tended to subvert public morals but also because it diverted the women's attention away from their patriotic duty of making clothing for the army. If they persisted in this easy way of raising funds, he suggested that the guilty parties open public gambling establishments staffed with professional card players and proceed "to fleece unwary patrons" with impunity.[23] Apparently this and many other scoldings had little effect, for lotteries continued to thrive until the close of hostilities.

Another favorite way of combining fun and purpose was that of holding public dinners and suppers. Recently discovered and long-neglected recipes were prepared, along with the unusual Southern staples, for a price. In making such projects successful scores of women emptied their smoke houses, gave up their tiny hoarded stores of coffee, and donated windfalls of scarce sugar and cream. On May 11, 1864, a Mobile group put on at the Odd Fellows' Hall a "Strawberry Supper" that included far more culinary delights than the berries cited in the advertisement. Specifically, customers had the choice of "a good gastronomic array of hams, turkeys, gumboes, chicken salad, ice creams, strawberries and cream in its multiform variety, Charlottes, custards, and floating islands, syllabubs and mountains of cake . . . coffee and other innocent liquids."[24] Ambitious rural cooks also sponsored dining festivities, as in the case of an 1864 Gainesville supper from which $1200 was taken in for the benefit of wounded soldiers serving in the armies of Generals Johnston and Forrest.[25]

During its short tenure as the Confederate capital, Montgomery's social life took on new dimensions. As throngs of Southern leaders gathered to build a new nation, the little city was hardly prepared to entertain such large numbers of solons and their wives, nor were the old families altogether happy with the new guests. For one thing, their own influence in social affairs was threatened by so many sophisticated outsiders, but even more threatening was the prospect of having their community contaminated by those who had lived in what was deemed the corrupt atmosphere of Washington, D.C.

> They could not get rid of their idea that Sodom had come to be imposed on them; and to their prejudiced nostrils there was an odor of sulphur in everything that savored of Washington society"

wrote Thomas C. DeLeon, the Mobile journalist and self-appointed chronicler of life in the first capital.[26] Even the well-born Mary Chesnut felt the pressure of local prejudice against strangers and she discovered that some Montgomery women registered marked signs of disbelief when told that there was no truth about "the awful things" attributed to Washington society. Time and again Mrs. Chesnut was asked her opinion of Montgomery, but, realizing it was a loaded question, she merely replied with "Charming! I find it charming."[27]

This deprivation of social intercourse with the natives forced the Confederate officials and their wives to seek each others' company in hotels or more frequently at social affairs held at the home of the first family. Here at the first White House Varina Howell Davis gave many receptions and gay dinner parties, with enough food and drink to founder the most fastidious guests. Here, too, came the wives of prominent Alabama leaders, not only for amusement but also to reminisce about mutual experiences in the old capital. Witty conversation and gossip were frequently mixed with political intrigue as these gatherings took on more and more the characteristics of a Confederate court. A few high-ranking Alabama office holders did open their homes to "the alien crowd," sometimes as a courtesy, but more often for the sheer fun of social discourse.

Moving in both circles was the ubiquitous Mary Chesnut, who looked disapprovingly upon certain high-living Alabamians and their overly ambitious wives. Heading her list was Aurelia Blassingame Fitzpatrick, the wife of Alabama's former United States senator and a noted beauty and hostess in her own right. The South Carolinian thought Aurelia too brazen a woman, because she had "poked Jeff Davis in the back with her parasol that he

might turn to speak to her" during the inauguration ceremonies. On another occasion Mary judged "the Fitzpatrick woman" as altogether too forward in her attempt
to secure a cabinet post for her husband, but when Mrs.
Fitzpatrick accused Davis of being "too gloomy" because
he spoke of a long war, Mrs. Chesnut politely passed the
remark off as an unintelligent interpretation of the president's words.[28]

Confederate Montgomery had much to offer fun-seek-
ers of the elite class. According to Thomas C. DeLeon,
the city sparkled with beautiful belles, who could be seen
at the splendid balls, dinner parties, and other festive
occasions given in private homes and in the city's few
luxury hotels. This gay boulevardier wrote in the most
extravagant prose in describing the charms and physical
appearance of the scions of old and respected families.
They were, moreover, all "fresh, frank, and fun-loving
girls" and one in particular, named Alice Vivian, "queened
it with the ripe royalty of Venus, Juno, and Minerva."
Another was dubbed "a raging, howling belle," and still
another, Ida Rice, was so popular that a cannon guarding
Charleston harbor was named in her honor.[29]

Montgomery's high society continued to entertain lav-
ishly even up to the last years of the war. Among the brilliant entertainments for which the home of Governor
Thomas Hill Watts was famed was the coming-out party
for his daughter during the 1864 social season. The signs
of war were hardly visible as splendidly dressed young
couples danced and dined until the early morning hours.
Nearly all of the city's elite were present, except one
woman who scornfully rejected her invitation with a curt
note stating that she "would not dance while Rome was
burning, though Watts, *et al.*—fiddled." But, the parties

nevertheless continued and large numbers showed up for Mary Given's debut festivities. After dancing until midnight, the guests were served a feast consisting of roast turkey, baked pig, tongues, hams, cakes, real coffee, and sugar. Shortly afterwards, Mary married a local swain and the groom's father presented his daughter-in-law with 300 bales of cotton.[30]

With the surrender of New Orleans in 1862, Mobile fell heir to much of the reputation for gaiety that had long been the exclusive monopoly of the Louisiana city. It was, in many ways, a natural legatee with an urban aristocracy, with French-flavored traditions, and it counted many citizens related by blood or marriage to the Crescent City's most socially prominent families. When some Creole aristocrats fled there as refugees they added luster to an already gala atmosphere and were warmly received by congenial hostesses eager to prove that Mobile was capable of being the second New Orleans of the South. There were great varieties of recreation available, but most highly favored of all were Mardi Gras balls, held either in private homes or public halls.

English author Fitzgerald Ross reported having the time of his life at one such affair and glowingly wrote that he found the reports "of the charm of the fair sex of Mobile . . . to be not at all exaggerated." He also accepted an invitation for a joy ride around Mobile Bay to inspect the Confederate defense installations. Among the guests were the governor, high ranking officers, and a party of young men and women. No sooner had the ship left the dock than a regimental band began playing dance music. When the merry-makers got halfway through a quadrille, Admiral Franklin Buchanan joined in and "created a great deal of confusion and merriment" by his dextrous execution of the dance. Ross noted that the admiral was a very popular figure among the pretty women, although in his opinion he was "ten years too young to be an admiral in England."[31] As was true of Montgomery, numerous balls were given for various charitable enterprises. Among the hundreds of this nature was one sponsored by the Hebrew Young Ladies' Society. Held in Temperance Hall on the evening of January 8, 1863, it was reported that "a happy throng . . . danced, waltzed, polkaed, and galloped" long past midnight.[32]

Mobile's reputation for high living drew fire from the critics. As social affairs showed no signs of abating, faultfinders began predicting that the city would fall an easy victim to enemy forces or incur the wrath of Divine Providence and be destroyed like the Biblical cities of Sodom and Gomorrah. According to Mrs. Dorian Hall of Lowndesboro, it was an alarming development that so "many of the ladies . . . are giving parties and are as gay as if there was no danger impending over them." The prudent country woman was especially shocked to learn that Mrs. Braxton Bragg led all others in playing the role of "a gay . . . butterfly and enjoying her husband's high position, and don't care for his fatigue after being on duty all day . . . he must go to parties and get up at 4 o'clock in the morning to attend to duties."[33] Others voiced similar complaints, but the vast majority of Alabama women were unaware of such gaiety or were too preoccupied with their own lives to care.

No doubt Mrs. Hall would have become even more disturbed if she had known of the elaborate salons kept by some of Mobile's social leaders. One of the most popular was presided over by Octavia Walton LeVert, the wife of a wealthy physician and the author of popular

travel books. Fond of society and dress, Octavia was one
of Alabama's most cultivated little creatures—well-
groomed, impeccably mannered, and fearless in the presence of strangers. It was said of her that "no stranger
with name or record could escape" an invitation to her
salon. At her Government Street mansion came generals
of the armies, admirals, colonels, priests, poets, authors,
and actors to mingle with each other in "a social jambalaya
not possible to match in Dixie."[34] For those preferring a
more sedate evening, there was the salon of Mary Walker
Fearn, also the wife of a wealthy doctor and a respected
civic leader. Hers became a kind of enclave of intellectuals
made up of such local literary lights as Theodore O'Hara,
Adelaide deVendel Chaudron, and Peter Hamilton. Here,
too, assembled members of Mobile's professional class
and descendants of "old French families."[35]

The wives of Alabama officials became conspicuous
figures in Richmond's high society and a few of them made
substantial contributions in enlivening the social scene for
amusement-starved Confederate office holders. Entertaining important dignitaries was easy for those who had acquired ample experience as hostesses in Washington before
the war. As noted by one New York journalist in 1904,
these antebellum hostesses were recognized for "their
natural and acquired graces . . . their inherited tastes and
ability in social affairs . . . [and it] was natural that the
reigns should fall to them."[36]

Virginia Clay was one of the most active figures in the
Richmond social scene during the early days of the war.
No stranger to society, this veteran hostess not only moved
in the inner circle of high-government wives, but was also
a frequent guest of such local aristocrats as the Iveses,
Lees, Harrisons, Warrens, and others claiming the dis-

tinction of belonging to the first families of Virginia. While making the rounds of fashionable parties, Mrs. Clay was given to elaborate dress and she rarely ventured into the evening in anything less resplendent than a complicated and majestic robe-de-style involving velvet and lace as well as satin.

The Alabama senator's wife was likely to be seen at every big affair, but the high point of her career came when she was cast in the role of Mrs. Malaprop in Sheridan's play, *The Rivals*. Staged at the Ives' home it was adjudged the most successful venture of the 1862 social season. According to several spectators, it was an event of dazzling brilliance, counting the president among the audience, along with other high-ranking dignitaries. Virginia was in her element, strutting on stage dressed in a rich brocaded gown, antique lace, jewels, and high puffed hair. Between acts during one performance she was not at all pleased with the audience's response and sent word that it should show more appreciation for the actors. Afterwards, it was reported that the cast was "fired by thunders of applause."[37]

As the war came closer, entertainments were drastically curtailed or canceled altogether, and the capital took on every aspect of a beleaguered city, with shortages of food and clothing manifest among all classes. Such a place had no charms for the fun-loving Mrs. Clay; although she did occasionally visit her husband in Richmond, she preferred living with friends and relatives in calmer sections of the Confederacy. Her forte was entertaining the mighty and it was not a time that had need of her services. Even her sister-in-law, Celeste Clay, conceded that the two of them "deserved *no credit for anything*. We have done *as* little for our country as any other two worthless women I

know."[38] Yet Celeste may have been too harsh in her estimate. It was, rather, an admirer of Mrs. Clay who came
close to recognizing her real value when he named his
daughter after Virginia and expressed the hope that when
the infant reached maturity she would "remember her
name sake, in all those truly womanly virtues and graces
. . . then we know that we will be proud of her."[39]

Other officials' wives, such as Mrs. John A. Campbell,
took an active part in Richmond's social life. She, too, had
acquired wide experience as an antebellum Washington
hostess as the wife of an associate justice of the Supreme
Court. After Justice Campbell accepted a position in the
Confederate Attorney-General's office, she maintained an
open house for entertaining important persons. The Campbell residence on fashionable Linton Row "was much
sought by the best of young and old," according to one
guest, not only because the hostess herself "was gentle and
delightful," but "the attractiveness of her grown daughters . . . was a magnet for the brave as well as gay." No
less popular was Mrs. Thomas J. Semmes, the wife of the
Louisiana senator and the former Myra Knox of Montgomery. Frequenting the Semmes home were Alabama
solons and army officers, where it was said they could
enjoy "a singularly notable 'mess' " in the company of
Vice President Stephens and other leading politicians.[40]
Bad health and the death of a son prevented Amelia Gayle
Gorgas from full participation in the society of Richmond,
but the wife of the Confederate ordinance chief did attend
a few receptions at the White House.[41]

Early in the war Alabama became a haven for thousands of refugees fleeing the invading armies in neighboring states. With very few exceptions most displaced persons lived a hand-to-mouth existence, depending in large

measure upon the charitable resources of their host communities.[42] A typical case was that of Elizabeth Avery Meriwether, who spent about a year of hard living in Tuscaloosa after having been banished from Memphis by federal authorities. In her own words this articulate woman described how her family of small children were forced to dwell "in a little rickerty 'tumble-down' house which seemed as if the wind might blow it away any day."[43] There were times when the family's larder consisted of "gresy hog meat" and other equally uninviting fare. On one occasion Mrs. Meriwether resorted to stealing corn from the garden of a prominent citizen in order to survive.[44] Hardship and frustration followed her relentlessly and, even after she had won a $500 prize for a book entitled *The Refugee*, the money was soon exhausted buying the highly inflated food items.[45]

However, a few affluent refugees found oases of plenty and luxury in remote corners of Alabama, and some even managed to recreate a gay and carefree style of living approaching the opulent days of the antebellum period. Such a colony existed at Tuskegee, where Frances Wallace found a haven after a long and difficult hegira from Kentucky. Here in 1864 she discovered "one of God's loveliest spots," with nothing to remind her of war except "the anxious hearts of Mothers and friends of men in the army." Despite these forebodings she joined in a round of parties, suppers, and dances given by local aristocrats and at the homes of members of the refugee colony. At one she was surprised to see "the ladies dressed in evening costume . . . some extravagantly dressed, and many glittered in their diamonds. . . . Nowhere in the South could you find more style," she wrote, "perhaps a greater variety, but nothing more; for wealth, style, beauty, and taste no place can surpass it, and this is the home of a refugee from Mississippi who claims to be only camping. . . ." Quite prophetically the Kentuckian concluded: "If this be a poor dying struggle, Oh! beautiful South, you are glamorous even in your death."[46]

9

My God! They are everywhere.

> Unless you have experienced it, one cannot know the
> horror, the unspeakable horror of the feeling of having
> the negroes run in the house and say: 'The Yankees
> are Coming!' That and the sound of cavalrymen wail-
> ing, the rowels of their spurs dragging on the floor, the
> clanking of their sabers will follow me like a nightmare
> to the end of my days.[1]

Thus wrote Rebecca Thompson Bayless in 1908, more
than forty years after a Federal raiding party entered her
plantation near Tuscumbia in northeastern Alabama. Suddenly it was invasion, and her reaction was typical of wom-
en who faced an enemy they never expected to see in their
homes.

Alabama did not perish in one cataclysmic crash, but
fell to Union forces in sections. The ordeal of war came
first to the northern areas, following the surrender of
Forts Henry and Donelson in neighboring Tennessee in
February of 1862. Nashville was next, and after the
Battle of Shiloh on April 6-7, the Tennessee Valley of
Alabama lay open to invasion by land and by river.[2] On
April 11, General O. M. Mitchell captured Huntsville
and in less than a week extended Union control from
Stevenson to Tuscumbia.[3] For the next three years there

168

was no peace in the valley as contending armies marched in and out burning and destroying, looting and pillaging the noncombatant population, sometimes from military necessity, but frequently from a spirit of malice as well as of revenge.

The coming of the enemy produced an atmosphere of uncertainty, apprehension, and confusion among the women of the conquered regions. Some had already chosen the precarious existence of refugeeing, but the majority remained at home and, for the most part, struggled alone in maintaining their families, private possessions, and personal dignity. For these the war now became an intimate part of daily living in which survival depended upon each individual's intelligence, diplomacy, and the employment of feminine stratagems in dealing with occupation forces. While the men were said to have accepted the situation with "patient endurance," the women became "morosely bitter" and were driven as "a point of honor," according to one Yankee observer, "to a foolish, yet absolute, devotion . . . to the Southern cause," and he credited them with "doing much to keep it alive."[4] It was an old story, as old as the history of invasion, but it was especially a story of women who exhibited hatred and sometimes open defiance of an enemy that intruded into their personal lives and forced an unwanted adjustment to a new order.

A good many articulate women kept records of their experiences; each one that did wrote as if posterity should know about the low character of the conquerors. Villification was their particular weapon, and, at the beginning, the fighting abilities of the Union forces came in for much ridicule despite their apparent successes. Immediately after the fall of Huntsville, one woman gave an unsparing satire of Northern troops as "truly a brave set" who had taken a city that was "strongly fortified with the most impenetrable brick houses, daring women, undaunted children and dubious bulldogs."[5] In an ecstasy of hate, Bettie Burrleson of Decatur portrayed the United States army to be nothing but "a band of ignorant . . . beastly and immoral men recruited from the riff-raff of cities" in the North. It was an incredible sight to see them camped on her front yard "thick as Pharo's frogs in Egypt," and to discover that none to whom she had talked possessed any schooling. But she was even more amazed that some had told her of their plans to desert rather than "fire another gun to free the negroes." Such a thought was strange to this woman who had always believed that emancipation was the sole war aim of all Northern soldiers.[6]

The whole idea of Yankees in Alabama was enough to drive patriotic women into paroxysms of rage, but the commanders of occupied towns came in for special denunciation. Among the first condemned everywhere was "that astronomical scoundrel, General O. M. Mitchell" while he was in command of Huntsville.[7] The scientist-soldier was held responsible for every real and imagined atrocity committed against the noncombatant population. "His career in our valley from beginning to end," wrote Virginia Clay, "was that of a martinet bent upon subjugation of the old and helpless and the very young, our youths and strong men being away in the field."[8] Virginia was really referring to her family's plight and that of other prominent families living in occupied areas.

The home of ex-Governor Clay became an object of suspicion and was kept under constant surveillance. It was frequently searched for arms and Confederate spies allegedly hiding there from authorities. The Clays also suffered great losses through confiscation, but the most costly loss was the burning of the family's 3,000-volume library.[9] Driven to desperation, the senior Mrs. Clay was once forced to seek relief from Federal sources, but when she discovered that it was necessary to admit being an "indigent person" she disdainfully refused that condition in obtaining food allotments.[10] The aging couple survived under the hardest conditions, and, as noted before, they were compelled to accept food from friends and finally to rent rooms for a living.[11]

Other families of leading Huntsville Confederates received similar treatment. The home of ex-Governor Reuben Chapman, where the family of Secretary of War Leroy P. Walker had gone for safety, was daily searched during the first occupation. In one instance a search party was "so scrupulous in their investigation that even the leaves of the dictionary were parted, lest the wily . . . Secretary should spirit himself between its covers." Cutglass decanters also were examined until the exasperated Mrs. Chapman could stand it no longer and inquired: "You don't expect to find General Walker in that brandy bottle, do you?"[12]

Although Huntsville's haughty *grande dames* scorned the occupying forces, they reserved a greater degree of hostility for Union sympathizers, or Tories, as such persons were commonly called by patriotic Confederates. Already excited by the presence of unwelcome invaders, feminine rebels became even more terrified of those "homemade Yankees" who donned the United States uniform and proceeded to search and confiscate private property. "Chief of these mauraders," according to Lila Greet, was a native of Madison County named Kinch Britz, who, on one occasion, attempted to enter her home only to have the door slammed in his face. After threaten-

ing to return at some future date and personally burn the
house, he left, but was shortly afterwards killed while
ransacking the house of a local citizen.[13]

The dread of Tories never abated but, if anything, was
intensified as the war stretched into years. It was the considered opinion of Mrs. C. C. Clay, Sr. that Southerners
everywhere, and especially those in Huntsville, would
have less cause to fear "if the traitors were out of the
country. . . ." She therefore supplied her son in Richmond
with a list of unionists whom she deemed dangerous to
the Confederate cause.[14] A no less charitable opinion was
held by a Mrs. Bierne, who saw Tories as devious characters. Every Tory of her acquaintance seemed over-anxious
to win loyal Southerners over to the Union side, and she
was also aware of their subterfuges of informing on Confederates, having them arrested, and then taking credit
for getting the hapless persons released from prison. "It
is humiliating enough to be compelled to ask a favor of
Yankees," she admitted, "but a thousand times worse to
ask anything of a Southern traitor." As for her, she
would rather die than seek aid from anyone except loyal
Confederates and she hoped that her fellow citizens
thought as she did.

Not every Huntsvillian had a brush with Tories, but
nearly every one came into contact with Union soldiers or
military officials at one time or another during the periods
of occupation. While most usually kept their thoughts private and treated their captors with supreme indifference,
there were those women who went out of their way in
demonstrating contempt for them. For the most part, such
gestures were harmless outbursts of bravado by over-
zealous patriots emboldened by the notion that females
were immune from harm because of their sex. For ex-

ample, when a squad of soldiers passed the residence of Mrs. Thomas Burton, she rushed out waving a Confederate flag and shouted in a loud voice: "Hurra for Jeff Davis & the Southern Confederacy!" Instead of resenting this display of chauvinism the men merely responded with brisk salutes and rode on.[15]

Others avoided contact by crossing streets upon seeing the approach of military pedestrians, and a few openly rejected the efforts of soldiers to be friendly. Major Moore of an Ohio regiment told of the time he barely escaped injury when he offered to close a carriage door for two women on a Huntsville street. As he grasped the handle "one of the termagants put forth her hand and pushed the door . . . violently shut" and almost caught his hand, but the startled officer regained his composure and politely observed: "Excuse me, I thought you were ladies," as they rode away in a pall of silence.[16]

However, there were instances when occupation authorities took action against anti-United States demonstrations. This was the case when two young girls were arrested for playing with hoops decorated with small rebel flags. The two were brought before the Provost Marshal, where they were interrogated but soon released with a stern warning not to display the flags in such a fashion in the future. This affair only served to harden resistance and was cited as a prime example of Yankee cruelty against defenseless women and children.[17]

Among the most vivid accounts of life in occupied Alabama was that of Mary Cook Chadick of Huntsville. Her diary began in the spring of 1862 with the Northern advance into her adopted homeland and ended in the summer of 1865 when she recognized that the war was over. Inevitably, however, in telling the story she is not politically impartial, for nothing she saw or heard shook for an instant her belief that the Confederacy and its inhabitants were in the right in their rebellion against the United States. On the contrary, the Massachusetts-born woman's loyalty increased in vigor and, as late as April of 1865, she tersely informed a Northern preacher, who had questioned her patriotism, that she was "the strongest Southern woman you ever saw."[18]

As the head of a household in a war zone, she was slated to experience many nerve-fraying days of uncertainty and fear. Like other wives of Confederate officers, her home was frequently searched, and there were those times in which she helplessly stood by as search parties confiscated prized possessions. On more than one occasion the Chadick house was commandeered to billet soldiers, leaving her and the children with only a few rooms in which to live. Hard, too, was the almost ceaseless movement of troops. The noise had an unnerving effect upon her and she once wrote that "their rattling wagons and clattering of hoofs ring on the ear from morning to night." Her peace of mind was not at all helped by the antics of drunken soldiers whom she once reported seeing "firing in the streets and endangering the lives of passerbys." On August 16, 1864, the frightened woman wrote that the town was full of drunks calling citizens from their houses, "accusing them of feeding bush-whackers or some such pretense, and then shooting them down."[19]

Despite the apparent dangers, this woman found that the hardest part of the war was being separated from her husband. Her diary is replete with expressions of yearning and she often missed him so much that it made her ill enough to require medical treatment. From time to time she visited Colonel Chadick whenever his regiment was stationed south of Huntsville in Confederate Alabama. In every case she endured great personal inconvenience and discomfort, but invariably considered such reunions worth the effort. Occasionally the colonel slipped through enemy lines for visits with his family. On one such occasion she displayed remarkable aplomb and courage in helping him to avoid capture when a search party suddenly appeared at the Chadick residence. She rushed to the front door and engaged the men in conversation while the rebel colonel ran out the back door and hid under a barrel in a neighbor's cellar. Later that evening she sent him civilian clothes by a friend to help him make his escape less conspicuous.[20]

Although life was hard, and at times unbearable, Mrs. Chadick discovered that all Yankees were not the brutes they were expected to be. In fact, she effected amicable relationships with individual soldiers and their wives while visiting in the homes of neighbors. At one gathering she made such a favorable impression that one Northern woman presented her with gifts of food and the latest issues of fashion magazines as tokens of friendship. Toward the end, she permitted her teen-age daughter to receive young officers and only registered mild protests when one suitor had an army band serenade the household. The most frequent caller was Captain John Fordyce, who won Mrs. Chadick's complete approval because he was "singularly handsome and gentlemanly in bearing and is highly popular with both friend and foe."[21] This "singularly handsome officer" later married the Chadick girl and at least one sectional chasm was bridged.

Life in other federally occupied towns of north Alabama was no less difficult. Here, too, women felt the brunt of war and came face to face with all the vicissitudes to

which an invaded land is heir. The small town of Athens
had been so devastated by troops under the command of
Colonel J. Basil Turchin that the Russian-born soldier
became the most hated man in Alabama. Even his superior
officer, General Don Carlos Buell, characterized his conduct as "a case of undisputed atrocity" and newspaper
editors everywhere condemned "the rape of Athens" and
asked, as did one in southeastern Alabama, that "swift
and retributive justice" be taken against the notorious
officer.[22] During the battle for Florence, Mrs. E. A.
O'Neal reported the frightening experience of having her
home fired on and afterwards entered by a drunken soldier
demanding whiskey or he would burn the house. After
dissuading him from doing so, she wrote her husband expressing the hope that "I will never see a *Yankee* again.
A horrible name to me."[23]

Similar scenes unfolded elsewhere, but the worst effects
of looting were felt by the mistresses of valley plantations
and farms. Alone and far removed from any semblance of
protection that could be requested of military authorities
located in urban areas, these women became victims of
robbery and rude treatment from stragglers of the main
army. The Greets of Madison County lost all their silver
except for a few pieces of cutlery that one member of the
family had hidden in her bosom. The sight of the strange
protrusions so amused the looters that they permitted her
to keep the treasure.[24] A more harrowing experience fell to
the Coleman family near Athens in 1864, when a clandestine group ransacked their home "from top to bottom
looting" and destroying furniture as well as other household items. When Mrs. Coleman pleaded with the man
whom she presumed to be in charge to stop the destruction, he replied with: "Damn you, I have no protection

for you—pitch into that home men and sack it."[25] The search for valuables continued for long wearying hours, after which the house was fired and the woman stood, forlornly, watching it burn as the men rode away shouting insults.

Other female heads of households fared as badly. "It must be that the worst part of the army were sent down into this valley," wrote J. B. Moore in 1863. "They took from widow ladies silver plate and watches, meat, broken open all houses that were closed, and robbed them of their contents." His mother-in-law had lost everything and this was especially galling, since she had opposed secession and had never contributed materially to the Confederate cause.[26] Ultimately, the Tennessee Valley was in shambles. During the brief period when Confederates controlled the region in 1863, one officer was shocked to find only "the site of some beautiful & elegant mansions with nothing but ashes & large rich plantations with the fences all burned & everything gone to waste & ruin."[27]

The collapse of Confederate defenses in north Alabama also produced the anguish of anarchy in the poorer hill and mountain sections south of the Tennessee River. Union cavalry raids swept over the area, destroying military objectives as well as civilian properties. Then a new violence threatened. Southern unionists banded together to fight Confederates and a frightful revenge was taken by both sides. Bandit groups also roamed the countryside, stealing, plundering, terrorizing women, torturing, and murdering both rebels and unionists—sometimes even slaughtering entire families.[28] Private and official records abound with accounts of atrocities committed against helpless females of the region. For example, it was reported that a Coosa County farm woman was first robbed of food supplies and then the bandit leader "abused her very much by seizing her by the throat until she was lifeless."[29] Law and order broke down so completely in several St. Clair County communities that many women were forced to flee "for protection to adjoining counties."[30]

Confederate partisans also committed gross outrages against Tory families. In 1863 General Grenville M. Dodge reported that scores of pro-Union citizens had been executed in Marion County and many others momentarily expected the same fate. He attested to the knowledge of a particular case involving the torture and murder of an elderly man and his daughter, while others were "hunted down by one hundred bloodhounds and captured." Over a thousand had been driven from their homes and were living in the forest "without food or shelter." And, that was not all. In addition, he knew of many more in hiding and waiting for an opportunity to escape their rebel oppressors.[31]

Even Confederate forces so debased themselves as to plunder their fellow citizens. One civilian of Lawrence County let the governor know that "the appearance of a body of Confederate cavalry fills every neighborhood with dread: and any man upon whose premises they camp regards himself as already ruined." He specifically accused the men in gray of "invading the privacy of families robbing the farms of their horses and mules, shooting down or driving off their stock . . . and committing every species of depredation which usually characterizes the march of a hostile army through a country subjugated by their arms."[32] North Alabama became a spectre of destruction at every turn and the senseless nightmare war stretched out night after night, month after month, and finally year after year until the end of the war.

Although the Civil War in Alabama, as elsewhere, was a conflict waged between male armies, there was a small and more or less unconventional body of women who chose to serve either the Confederacy or Northern causes as spies, guides, and saboteurs. None were trained agents in the modern sense of the term nor did any seem to have special commissions from their respective governments. They were mere amateurs who took advantage of the presumed protection afforded by their sex and were swept up in the excitement of the moment and performed impulsive acts of heroism. A case in point was that of Mrs. W. D. Chadick, who made frequent entries in her diary that strongly suggest that she passed military information on to her husband in the Confederate army. Most of the data was gathered in Huntsville and was based on her personal observations, or upon information supplied by friends and relatives. For instance, on July 5, 1862, she noted that 15,000 Federal troops were encamped outside of town and were probably headed for Chattanooga in a few days. Scarcely two days later the observant woman dispatched her husband a letter by way of a close friend who had permission to cross the lines into Confederate Alabama. It is not unlikely that she included the aforementioned information in this correspondence. On several other occasions she sent letters through the lines after having first recorded detailed military information in her diary.[33]

Very little is known of the activities of Union spies except those fleeting references pertaining to their services found in the official records of United States army officers. In 1864, for example, when it was vital to know the exact place Confederate General John Bell Hood's army intended crossing the Tennessee River en route to Nashville, "a Union woman" of Huntsville sent in to Union authorities the information that the "rebels were ordered to prepare five days rations" as a clue to a Huntsville crossing.[34] Another, identified only as "a Union lady" from Decatur, wrote that no large concentration of Southern troops were in her town, only "an occasional straggler," and reported no knowledge of the location of the main body of Hood's command.[35] More concrete information did come into Union headquarters from "a Lady of Florence" who told of "the rebels . . . trying to pontoon the river at Bainbridge . . . and they are fortifying to protect the crossing . . ." at that point.[36]

A few high-spirited young girls took dangerous chances in helping the Confederate war effort. Lila Greet was one of these and the high point of her career came in 1864 when she accompanied a demolition squad to destroy a railroad bridge on the Tennessee River. "With my own little brown hand," she wrote in later years, "I applied the torch . . . and we thus detained the supplies for a whole division of the Yankee army."[37] Although Miss Greet's activity went unnoticed by the state at large, there was at least one teen-age girl who received widespread acclaim for her role in helping Southern forces to capture a Northern raiding party. This was Emma Sansom, who led General Nathan B. Forrest to a ford on Black Creek near her Etowah County home in 1863 and thus enabled the pursuing Confederates "to overcome a very formidable obstacle . . . and gained . . . at least three hours in time" to overtake General A. D. Streight's command.[38] In recognition of her services, the legislature in 1863 awarded her a gold medal and in 1899 deeded her a tract of land, together with the title of "the heroine of Alabama."[39]

While contending armies performed their ceaseless wheeling and swooping over the blasted terrain of north Alabama, nearly two-thirds of the state remained untouched by invasion. But the final months of the war became a period of almost uninterrupted disaster for central Alabama as the United States intensified its assault to bring the war to a close. The drive into the heart of the rich Black Belt section was launched by General James H. Wilson in the spring of 1865. Starting at Chickasaw in Lauderdale County, he drove relentlessly southward without meeting serious opposition. At Elyton, he sent part of his command to take Tuscaloosa, which fell an easy victim on April 4, 1865. Military stores were promptly destroyed and the state university fired as a prize of war.[40] Despite strict orders against looting, the homes of noncombatants were entered, and, according to one observer, "the Yankees took as much provisions as they could carry off. . . ."[41]

Farther south, Wilson won a decisive victory near Selma and the most important munitions center of Alabama was entered on April 2. As the army took possession of strategic positions, the streets of the little city were swirling with citizens helplessly confused and fleeing in all directions. As elsewhere, some troopers seized private property and dealt ruthlessly with any kind of resistance. Some broke into private residences, seizing valuables and demanding alcoholic beverages of badly frightened women. But soldiers generally ignored civilians and went about the business of destroying arsenals, foundries, and other legitimate prizes of war. At least Ella Smith, a recent graduate of Judson College, thought that "the reports of the treatment of . . . Selmians . . . are much exaggerated." Although her home had been taken over as a hospital, during that time she reported not hearing "an uncivil word" from Yankees. In fact, the only damage the Smiths suffered was a cannon ball lodged in a front porch column, which the family agreed to preserve "as a token of Fed friendship."[42]

Outlying plantations were broken into, but many mistresses had already taken the precaution of hiding treasured possessions. Silver service sets, jewelry, and a great variety of small heirlooms were carefully buried in flower gardens or entrusted into the hands of faithful slaves. Some, however, delayed, as was the case of one woman who was in the process of hiding her engagement ring in a vegetable garden just as a party of Yankee stragglers appeared at the front gate. Unaware of her action, the household slaves, under questioning, revealed that valuables might be found in that garden. The men spent the better part of a day digging, but failed to find anything. Then they began searching the house, but when a pet peacock began crowing the searchers mistook the sounds for rebel yells and hastily fled the premises.[43] Most plantations and farms were plundered of chickens, livestock, and the contents of smoke houses. At Sarah Ellen McIllwain's place "a regular warfare was waged upon the feathered tribe . . . with chickens flying, turkeys running, dogs barking and Yankee shouts a regular panic was enacted in the back yard," she later wrote of a Yankee looting.[44]

Between Selma and Montgomery the approach of Wilson's army filled women with terror and many frantically went about hiding valuables. At Hayneville the homes of the affluent were ransacked, trunks broken open, feather mattresses ripped open and scattered as though caught up in a hurricane. Nearly every smoke house was divested of hams, bacon, and other edibles.[45] In neighboring Prairieville the people were struck numb with terror and locked themselves in their houses. In fact, they were so terror-stricken that the Episcopal rector had to conduct one burial service at night and use slave pallbearers because the friends of the deceased refused to come, or had fled.[46]

The surrender of Montgomery was accomplished with little resistance or bloodshed on April 12. Here at last Yankees were in the "Cradle of the Confederacy!" and, it was strange for one woman to see "the blue coats—looking brilliant with buttons and *'accoutrements'* " parading up Market Street heading for the capitol.[47] Wilson lost no time in issuing orders prohibiting looting and soon large numbers of women appeared at headquarters requesting that guards be posted at their residences.[48] Nevertheless, there were some minor cases of stealing and confiscations by clandestine bands of soldiers. A considerable number of families lost their milk cows, but the hardest hit were nursing mothers. A local physician took it upon himself to ask for General Wilson's assistance in getting the animals returned to women with infants. He explained that four hundred patients under his care were without milk because "your coming here so alarmed and excited them that all their milk had dried up and they must have their cows back."[49] Although the records do not reveal what action was taken, it is highly unlikely that Wilson remained cold to the doctor's argument.

In March of 1865 turbulence and conflict embraced south Alabama as United States forces moved ever closer to the city of Mobile. Just as everywhere else, many civilians had fled, but most stayed on simply because there was no place of refuge left. Among those remaining was the Waring family, whose daughter, Mary, kept a diary of the exciting events of the beleaguered city. At first she was greatly disturbed by the roar of cannons, but soon adjusted to the sounds and amused herself as best she could by watching gunboat engagements through a telescope from a relative's second-floor window. When not viewing the spectacles of war, this teen-age rebel caught up on her reading, faithfully attended music lessons, and rolled bandages for wounded soldiers.

Finally, the noises of battle ended. Confederate defenses crumbled at every point and on April 10 the city's alarm bell announced that the siege was over. This rendered Miss Waring inconsolable, and she stayed at home during the victory parade through the city. The following day she ventured out to see "the hated Yankees" and wrote that they were "the commonest, dirtiest-looking set I ever saw," but at the same time she found them "very quiet and orderly. . . ."[50] With the fall of Mobile, Alabama's days in the Confederacy came to an end, except for some mopping-up operations in the southeastern region of the state. Raids into that section originated from the port city and Montgomery. In one such operation into Eufaula, the troops under their leader, General Benjamin H. Grierson, swarmed all over the place and caused one woman to exclaim in unbelieving dismay: "My God! They are everywhere!"[51]

Much has been written about the loyalty of slaves during the war, but on those frequent occasions when they experienced invasion their loyalty varied widely from individual to individual. At first the war was viewed as a white man's affair in which they had no direct involvement, but gradually it dawned on them that they did have a vital stake in its outcome. The Emancipation Proclamation of 1863 heightened this realization, and as Union forces widened their control thousands of Negroes deserted to the enemy. According to one Union officer· stationed in Huntsville, many became "confident that the rainbow and the bag of gold were in the camps of the Federal army."[52] The mask of loyalty was torn away at last and dismayed mistresses such as Mrs. Chadick rationalized that Negro slaves were duped into leaving "their real friends" by mischievous soldiers and army chaplains.[53] Others felt as did Tillie Houston of Leighton when she expressed pity for slaves who had gone over to the army. She predicted that Northern abolitionists would surely "let . . . a poor negro starve . . . at their doors or will be willing to sell them to Spaniards in Cuba."[54]

On the other hand, some slaves exhibited great loyalty and remained with their owners throughout the invasion. Most of these were house servants, passionately attached to mistresses, whose loyalty constituted one of the most cherished traditions in family records in the years ahead. There were instances in which slaves helped mistresses escape when the invasion began and others who rendered valuable assistance in hiding family possessions. In rare cases slaves even shared their owners' contempt for the enemy. One, named Bert, struck a blow for the Confederacy by filling the canteens of Yankee soldiers with water from a hog trough, and tightened the caps very tightly so as to remove all trace of the unwholesome contents. To carry the ruse a step further, she gave them fresh pails of water to sufficiently slake their thirst so that it would not become necessary to open the canteens of foul water until much later.[55]

Some took an instant dislike to the Yankees, mainly because they were made to perform extra work and suffered the loss of food along with their mistresses. Cheney Cross, a slave living near Evergreen in 1865, reminisced in later years how she was forced to mount a ladder and throw meat from her mistress' smoke house. "I kept throwing out Miss Mary's hams and sausages until they holler, 'Stop.' " At this order she came down the ladder "like a squirrel, and I ain't stop backing til I reach Miss Mary." Then she and her mistress watched the destruction of property and mournfully remarked that when the soldiers left "the whole place was strewed with mulitation." Hanna Irwin, a slave witness of invasion at Eufaula, expressed a similar opinion, but spoke more emphatically of the enemy. Yankees were, to her, "all right in their place . . . but they never belonged in the South."[56]

10

I had no idea it would ever result this seriously.

The Civil War permeated the life of every Alabama woman and affected everything she did and thought. With very few exceptions it was a personal war in which most had too much invested to consider it in any other light. In the bleak four years to Appomattox their menfolk fought in the armies and they had involved themselves in practically everything related to the war effort except military duty. They shared equally in the exultations over the new nation's victories and, along with the men, lamented its defeats. Like the soldiers in gray, they also became weary of war and went into periods of deep depression and finally lost the will to win.

In a recent study, Bell I. Wiley states that Southern morale began waning in the winter of 1861-1862 "under the dampening effects of the first military reversals, disillusionment with high leadership and the dawning prospects of a long, hard conflict." And, even though prospects for success were raised for a time during the summer of 1864, Wiley concludes that Lincoln's reelection, plus the continuing battlefield reverses of Southern arms, coupled with a

deepening discontent with the government and an unprecedented burden of hardship and war weariness brought a flood of despair in the fall and winter of 1864-1865 which reduced the fire [of enthusiasm] to smouldering coals and finally quenched it altogether.[1]

These and a multitude of other factors had a profound effect in lowering civilian morale and long before the shooting strated some of the more perceptive Alabama women envisioned a hard road to independence, or at worst a hopeless venture. Many must have felt as did Sarah R. Espy of Cherokee County when she wrote in her diary on March 19, 1861: "I feel badly for when the war commences . . . I fear our happy days are all gone." A year later the pessimistic Mrs. Espy's fears were strengthened by the capture of Nashville. Out of this bleak prospect she wrote: "This is a dreadful stroke on us; it seems that our enemy will overrun us."[2] Shortly afterwards her plantation was overrun and her thoughts turned toward peace at almost any price. Equally unhappy about the war was Jesse Webb, who wrote her husband from Greensboro soon after the summer victory at First Manassas, praying that "those Yankees could be persuaded to make peace—but I fear they will not until they are well whipped and I now fear that will be hard work for our few men."[3]

A crushing sense of depression seized women everywhere as their men left for the fighting fronts. The sudden realization that men could get killed plunged many into deep gloom and they began to question the wisdom of the independence movement. On December 9, 1861, Martha Shorter wrote to a friend how painful it was for her to contemplate the four months' absence of her "handsome noble-hearted husband." She could hardly bear the thought of his becoming "a target for those contemptable Yankees," and regretted not having the same fortitude of

making the "great sacrifices for Southern Independence"
as that which animated her mother-in-law.[4]

Mary Williamson expressed similar feelings and the
prospect of her husband's entering the army sent her into
paroxysms of despair. For weeks before he left she wept
alone at night and spent many waking hours meditating
over the dubious value of the war. When he finally departed she mournfully wrote in her diary that "this great
sorrow makes me forget I ever had such a feeling as
patriotism. . . ." The distraught woman never knew any
peace of mind thereafter, and was led to write: "It seems
this war is destined to last a long time. I had no idea it
would ever result this seriously."[5]

Mothers of army-age sons suffered no less anguish and
lived in dread of the day of farewells. Some managed to
keep up a stoical front until after the leavetaking was
over; then they broke down into uncontrollable fits of
weeping. While on a visit to Alabama relatives, Fannie
Beers wrote feelingly of one such scene that she had witnessed:

> Walking towards the house where I was to await con-
> veyance to the plantation of my uncle, I heard the
> moaning of one apparently in deep distress. At the door
> the lady of the house appeared with red eyes and a
> sorrowful countenance. Said she, 'Just listen at Mrs.
> ————. Her son went off on the boat to join the army,
> and 'pears like she can't get over it.' *She kept up splen-
> did until after he got off.'*

For a moment Fannie thought of offering some words of
comfort, but decided it best "not . . . to intrude upon
such sorrow." Later on, during a subsequent visit, Mrs.
Beers encountered "the horrors of suspense" that were

manifest among scores of rural women over the welfare of their soldier relatives. "Every day—every hour," she observed, "was frought with anxiety and dread. Rumor was always busy, but they could not hear *definitely;* they could not know how their loved ones were faring." And, she continued: "Ghastly vision made night hidious. During the day, the quick galloping of a horse, the unexpected appearance of a visitor, would agitate a whole household, sending women in haste to some secret place where they might pray for strength to bear patiently whatever tidings the messenger should bring."[6]

Expressions of woe and prayers asking for God's intervention in behalf of peace proliferated in letters and diaries as women everywhere agonized over the fate of their men in the army. Frequently, many became especially morose after the return of relatives to duty following furloughs. In 1862, when Martha Jane Crossley's brother left Perote after a short leave, she gave up to crying and musing about the prospects of peace. On more than one occasion she also expressed concern for all Confederate soldiers. For example, the sight of frost one winter morning brought to mind "the whiter snows which are falling around our poor destitute soldiers on the borders all these days" and made her sad, and she wept and prayed for an early end of the war.[7]

By 1864, the morale of Perote women had reached such a low level that one visiting soldier wrote that "the ladies were becoming despondent of our ultimate success in the war."[8] Nothing he said or did seemed to rekindle their earlier enthusiasm and hopes of a Southern victory. They had had enough of war, their men had been killed, wounded, and captured, and now they only wanted peace.

Although despondency gripped other communities,

many individual women's moods changed with the ebb and flow of the South's military fortunes. No doubt many experienced the same elation as Mary Williamson over the news that the "iron-clad vessel, the *Merrimac,* played the wild with the *Yankee fleet*" in the spring of 1862. Yet, many also must have been just as apprehensive as she was about impending battles in Virginia and elsewhere. On the eve of the Battle of Chickahominy she was so dispirited that she literally cried out in her diary: "Oh! as I write I could scream from *anguish.* Despair is almost preferable to this suspense; . . . we have heard nothing particular from the Boys, it seems impossible for them all to be spared." When news reached her that "the Boys" had survived, she "shouted from joy," but not for long. Information of other battles plunged her into the same mental anguish and she prayed that "God in mercy grant that with the dawn of another month may come the *glad tidings of peace.*"[9] The surrender of Vicksburg and Port Hudson in 1863 produced "a gloomy time" at Northport, according to Mrs. S. C. Cain, and made her fear that "the Yankees will be here in a short time and if they come I recon they will burn us up."[10]

As was to be expected, the women's morale was severely weakened by the death of relatives. Battle casualties were sometimes sent home in pine coffins and mourning weeds became a common sight throughout the state. Women could be seen scanning death lists posted on bulletin boards or nervously guiding their fingers down the list of deaths appearing in newspapers. Many a woman rushed over to console a neighbor upon hearing of a death in the family. It was a high and terrible price for women to pay for independence and it rendered many inconsolable and permanently depressed. It eroded the morale of those personally affected and, for others, even the first blood made "all hearts . . . anxious" in the small town of Marion after the funeral of a local soldier whose body had been sent there for interment.[11] Even the war-hardened nurse, Kate Cumming, succumbed to feelings of despair as she viewed the carnage on the battlefield of Chickamauga. "Oh! what a fratricide was there!" she wrote; "it makes one cry out in anguish . . . 'Peace! peace! when will it come?' "[12]

The desire for peace became especially strong during the traditional holidays. For Mrs. Chadick, wartime Christmases were sad occasions, with little of the Christian meaning of "Peace on earth and good will toward men," but New Years' celebrations were even sadder. Of January 1, 1865, she wrote:

> What a contrast between this and a New Year's morning five years ago, before the advent of this miserable war! When each day brings with it such terrible and startling events, what may be the record of the coming year? I dread to think of it.[13]

High hopes and courage are no substitutes for strength, and public morale waned perceptibly as waves of Union armies entered north Alabama, smashing every pocket of resistance. But, worse than invasion itself, was the loss of faith that some women had previously put in their Confederate defenders. The failure of General Phillip D. Roddy to drive the enemy from the Tennessee Valley caused many to despair of ever being rescued. "The Defender of North Alabama" was once characterized by a woman of that region as "a poor Confederate soldier who would bluster up and fire a few shots," and then retreat so as to allow Yankee forces to confiscate the civilians' cotton, which she claimed was later shared with Roddy.[14] To Mrs. E. A. O'Neal it was a serious mistake to retain this general in command and if he was not soon replaced by a more competent officer, she predicted that "we will have the Yankees frequently."[15] Before long the unsuccessful general and his command became the object of ridicule among the valley people. "It is a standing joke here," related one woman of Franklin County, "that Roddy's men spend their whole time hunting their horses or buttermilk. The 'buttermilk cavalry' and 'Life Insurance Concern' are two of their common names."[16]

As the years passed without relief from occupation, humorous references drew little laughter from war-wracked inhabitants of north Alabama. The noncombatants showed signs of utter despair and one contemporary female confided in her diary that: "We are in a dreadful strait, that is certain and none but an Almighty Army can save us; we might as well be trying to become reconciled to our unhappy destiny."[17] Hope, too, began to fade of "an Almighty Army" coming from Europe. Virginia Clay was adversely affected by William L. Yancey's failure to get aid from abroad. In 1862 she took note of his depressed appearance and said that: "Every action and each word he uttered demonstrated that he knew and felt the ultimate downfall of the Confederacy."

Mrs. Clay also witnessed, and doubtlessly came under the influence of, her close friend Lucius C. Q. Lamar's dire prediction that "our cause was hopeless," after his unsuccessful mission to involve European nations on the side of the Confederacy.[18] Alabama Congressman William R. Smith also foretold the downfall of the Southern republic if European intervention was not forthcoming. In fact, he wrote his wife back in 1862 that "nothing can save us but European interference and if withheld, there is no contemplating the horrors of the future of this generation."[19]

The slightest reminder of better days had a doleful effect upon women of the homefront and cast many into helpless feelings of despair and defeatism. "I miss you more than ever," said Mary Fitzpatrick in a letter to her husband from the family plantation in 1862; "these old oaks, this house, in fact everything is so associated with you; in vain I look around for you; Oh Phillips when will it end." Earlier she had told of her father's elaborate preparations for hiding slaves and food supplies in case of invasion and defeat.[20]

Even inanimate objects evoked a yearning for the days of peace. In explaining that the fancy stationery used in an 1863 letter to her husband was the last of prewar supplies, Wilhelmine Easby-Smith meditated on the calamitous effects of the war. She wrote that "once we were a proud, happy, prosperous nation," and went on to ask, "What are we now? What shall be nine years hence?" Her answer to the last question was possible defeat and she predicted that at some future date "another Gibbon may be writing the rise and fall of the *Great Republic* of the West and Freedom, Liberty, and Self-government will be 'among the things that were.' "[21]

The corrosive effects of defeatism began manifesting themselves among both sexes in a score of ways by 1863 and even the most ardent Confederates openly expressed their disillusionment in those leaders responsible for bringing about the independence movement. In 1863 a Montgomery carpenter en route through enemy lines told Union General W. S. Rosecrans that many capital city citizens were already "tired of war, some in favor of giving up no matter which way it goes." In fact, he knew many who were "very much down on W. L. Yancey, and blame[d] him with bringing these troubles on."[22]

During the same year, Sarah Follandsbee wrote of hearing "the first *grumblings* about the war, wishing it were ended, even with concessions." At a dinner party in Montgomery this teacher also told of overhearing a male guest denounce Yancey "as the instigator of secession [*and*] the cause of all current troubles."[23] Others lost faith in high military leaders such as Lee, Beauregard, and Polk, but most of the complaints were focused on Confederate political leaders in Richmond. Octavia Levert, chafing under continuing defeats, wrote on March 18, 1863: "Oh! why, why, does Davis continue to adhere to his defensive policy. Let us strike boldly and we shall succeed. We must succeed—our cause is just and God will make the right prosper."[24]

As previously noted, others complained of timid leadership, but there were some who laid the blame on Alabama's aristocratic class. In northern Franklin County, Virginia Williamson singled out the "stay-at-home gentry" for much of the calamities befalling the Confederacy. "I don't believe in the passive patriotism of so many of our 'chivalry' have possessed," she wrote in her diary. "Hurrahing for Jeff Davis and Beauregard is well enough, but staying at home and doing nothing else is bad, bad."[25]

Amazingly enough, neither Confederate nor state governments gave much attention to checking the ever-sinking spirits of the civilian population. In fact, no official propaganda program existed aside from that of executive proclamations expressing gratitude for women's war work and frequent calls for days of prayer and fasting. Yet, of some help were the private endeavors of editors and ministers who hammered at the dangers of racial amalgamation and depicted the horrors of defeat in the event of a Union victory. Some servicemen exhorted their women-folk back home to be of good cheer, as was the case of J. W. A. Sanford when he wrote his dispirited mother on July 15, 1863, to "Cheer up. 'The night is far spent, the day is at hand.' The war cannot endure many years, it may end in a few months." He continued: "The enemy cannot subdue us. Our independence will be established and our liberties secured," and he lapsed into scripture with the quotation: "For the Lord shall comfort Zion; he will comfort all her waste plains; and he will make her wilderness like Eden and her desert like the garden of the Lord; joy and gladness shall be found therein, thanksgiving and the voice of melody."[26]

Many other soldiers wrote relatives along the same lines, but there were those who criticized entire communities for their lack of confidence in the Confederate cause. In a lengthy letter to the *Clarke County Democrat* in 1864, a discharged soldier blasted "croakers and submissionists" of both sexes for "loving their gains . . . better than their independence." Such persons were deserving of no sympathy, particularly since they had "plenty to eat, and are hundreds of miles distant from the enemy" and had every reason to count their blessings and therefore should lend more effort toward backing the struggle for independence.[27]

During the final months of the war desperate measures were undertaken by unwavering optimists to raise civilian morale. Again, the press and preachers intensified their exhortations with guarantees of ultimate Southern victory if only the people would strive harder in backing the war effort. Embittered Confederates rushed to print, flooding newspapers with accounts of Yankee atrocities allegedly committed against noncombatants since the start of the war and predicted that the same fate awaited Alabamians if the state fell to the enemy. But, as the situation worsened, more tangible efforts came into being. Out of a mass meeting held at Mobile in late February, 1865, emerged an organization known as "The Society of Loyal Confederates," with the avowed purpose of "promoting, in the Confederacy, a spirit of hopeful, ardent, and devoted patriotism."[28]

In a letter endorsing this group one citizen called upon all Southern women to help out by "sewing, knitting, spinning, weaving, and if necessary, like the German women of the Thirty Years' War, perform all kinds of manual labor." He also admonished them to "drive laggards back to the field . . . rebuke the coward's words . . . inspire with hope the heart almost ready to sink under the trial and suffering . . . to check extravagant expenditures in foreign articles, which appreciate the currency of our enemy to the ruin of our own." Women everywhere could do these things and much more such as giving up "every piece of jewelry and plate they have, to sustain our government in prosecuting the war and improve our finances." They could, he concluded, "pay their part of the price of liberty, which is not only external vigilance, but also endurance, and sacrificial effort. All this they can do. All this they will do! And future ages will point back to the noble deeds of Southern women with unrequited admiration."[29]

A very large order indeed, but in reality it was too late —the will to win had already taken leave and stirring appeals had little meaning to a frightened population girding themselves for invasion. Even those patriots living abroad sensed the futility of continuing hostilities. At least Martha F. Crawford thought so as she wrote the following lament on March 31, 1865, while serving as a missionary in China: "For four years our land has been given over to war. Three brothers . . . have been in the army fighting for their homes. The cruel invader has been devastating through the length and breadth of our once quiet happy land. In mind I have seen and felt it all."[30] She too had become despondent and recognized that the South had lost its struggle for independence.

The realization that the end was at hand came hard to die-hard Confederate women. A few totally rejected reality and as late as the first two weeks of April in 1865 Mrs. Chadick continued to discount the news of military reverses as mere Yankee rumors. This unyielding patriot categorically refused to believe it possible for the Confederacy to fall and wrote in her diary on April 13, 1865:

> If there was any truth in the late news [Lee's surrender] Huntsville would be vocal with shouts of joy! Who knows but after all the star of the Southern Confederacy is in the ascendant! We will say to you in confidence, dear journal, right here that we in the Yankee lines have become so thoroughly accustomed to those lying rumors that, when they actually tell us the truth, we don't believe them.

However, the following day Lee's surrender was corroborated and while mass demonstrations of joy were taking place in the streets outside of her home, Mrs. Chadick capitulated and wrote the simple statement of being "heartsick and thoroughly disgusted with everything."[31]

The collapse of the Confederacy had a profound effect upon Alabama's articulate women. To some it was viewed as a calamity from which they thought it impossible to recover. The sacrifices, the heartbreak, and thought of all the hard work, seared Augusta Evans's mind with an indelible hatred for Yankees. She was bitter and unyielding. Even two years after the war she refused to receive Federal officers into her home and wrote her reasons for not doing so:

> Having been an ardent and conscientious secessionist, and *indulging still* in an unwavering faith in the justice and sanctity of the principles for which we fought and prayed so devotedly, I of course could not find it agreeable to associate with these, who are arrayed in arms against my own section and people.[32]

But for others, and perhaps the majority, the Civil War had been a hard fight, fought fairly by both sides, and their side had lost honorably. And, although reconciliation would be difficult, it was necessary for the living to carry on and forget the rancors engendered by the war. Behind them was defeat and humiliation, but before them was a future as united Americans. No doubt a great many must have thought as Kate Cumming did when she soliloquized about the end of the Confederacy:

> This year has developed the fate of the South. Time has revealed the utter loss of all our hopes. A change must pass over every political and social idea, custom, and relation. The consummation makes the year just passed ever memorable in our annals. In it gathers all the interest of the bloody tragedy; from it begins a new era, midst poverty, tears, and sad memories of the past. Oh, may we learn the lesson that all this is designed to teach; that all things sublunary are transient and fleeting. . . . And forgetting the past, save in the lessons which it teaches let us . . . redeem the time, live humbly, and trust God for future good. . . .[33]

Thus the Civil War ended on a double note of bitterness for some and optimism for future good to others. In retrospect it brought out more of the best than the worst in thousands of Alabama women and in a great variety of ways affected their lives as no other event in the history of the state. Rich and poor alike were caught up in a conflict that they regarded as much their war as did the men who fought the battles and managed the affairs of government. Their thoughts and actions demonstrated this beyond contest. Many took an inconspicuous but definite hand in promoting secession and in building the new nation. As willing participants in the struggle for independence a heretofore homebound population helped in raising armies, formed auxiliaries in behalf of the war effort, and labored incessantly in caring for sick and wounded soldiers. The less inhibited and better educated struck out against apparent injustices in a way few would dare consider undertaking during less troublesome times. They also performed men's work, experienced severe economic privation with a minimum of complaint, and took time out to provide consolation and amusement for their beloved warriors. Scores experienced the brunt of invasion with all its accompanying horrors and destruction and finally, like the men, became weary of war, lost faith in the Confederacy, and gave up.

Despite their contributions, the Civil War did little to free Alabama women from their traditional place in society. In the years ahead only a fortunate few could take advantage of the new opportunities open to women in school teaching or afford the luxury of involvement in such postwar activities as temperance crusades, agrarian organizations, and the women's rights movement. Most were either too apathetic or too deeply preoccupied with survival as the wives of poor whites, tenant farmers, and share-croppers to bother with social ferment. Shaken and scared by the leveling experience of Reconstruction and sharing the principles of reigning Bourbon politicians, the upper-class woman settled for the prewar status of just being a "lady," and, as such, left the management of public affairs to men. When the prestigious Alabama Federation of Women's Clubs came into existence in 1895, its first president made it patently clear that "we are not reformers in any sense of the word, nor is it a part of our purpose to disturb the public equilibrium," but, "our target is mental culture."[34] And, although the women's suffrage movement touched Alabama at the close of the century, its impact was light—almost imperceptible; women got the vote only through the ratification of the Nineteenth Amendment by other states.[35]

Although Alabamians turned away from progressive reforms, their loyalty to the Confederacy persisted through the remainder of the nineteenth and well into the twentieth century. Fealty to the lost cause has been especially strong among the state's women and the guns of war had hardly cooled before commemorative exercises honoring the war dead came into being throughout Alabama. At first women's auxiliaries formed an essential as well as a conspicuous part of Confederate veterans' organizations, but it was not long before they established a separate group under the name of the United Daughters of the Confederacy. This organization became involved not only in philanthropic and educational projects, but in addressing itself to the "vital" issues of the past have done much toward making the Confederacy a glorious failure.

Notes

Chapter 1

1. Mary Elizabeth Massey, *Bonnet Brigades* (New York, 1966), p. 3.
2. William Garrett, *Reminiscences of Public Men in Alabama for Thirty Years* (Atlanta, 1872), pp. 314–15.
3. *Eighth Census of the United States, 1860, Manufacturing* (Washington, 1865), p. 13.
4. Minnie Clare Boyd, *Alabama in the Fifties: A Social Study* (New York, 1931), p. 110.
5. *Ibid.,* pp. 119, 122.
6. Quoted in William Perry Fidler, *Augusta Evans Wilson, 1835–1909: A Biography* (University, Alabama, 1951), p. 67. Hereafter cited as *Augusta Evans Wilson.*
7. Rollin G. Osterweis, *Romanticism and Nationalism in the Old South* (New Haven, 1949), p. 88.
8. See John Witherspoon DuBose, *The Life and Times of William Lowndes Yancey* (Birmingham, 1892), pp. 297–310 and *passim* and Austin L. Venable, "William L. Yancey's Transition from Unionism to States Rights," *Journal of Southern History* 10 (August, 1944) : 341–42.
9. *Weekly Herald* [Benton], September 6, 1860, quoting the *Montgomery Daily Advertiser* and the *New Orleans Bee,* n.d.
10. Mrs. E. P. Lee to Sue Smith, June 24, 1854, Washington M. Smith Papers, Manuscript Division, Duke University.
11. Journal of Sarah R. Espy (Typescript in Alabama Department of Archives and History), Montgomery, Alabama.
12. *Montgomery Daily Mail,* January 28, 1860.
13. *Ibid.,* March 8, 1860.
14. *Acts of the General Assembly of Alabama* (1860), pp. 14–15.
15. *Montgomery Daily Mail,* March 16, 1860.
16. *Ibid.,* March 17, 1860.
17. Ralph A. Wooster, *The Secession Conventions of the South* (Princeton, 1962), pp. 63–64.
18. *Florence Gazette,* January 16, 1861, quoting the *North Alabamian,* n.d.
19. *Montgomery Daily Mail,* March 8, 1860.
20. *Montgomery Weekly Mail,* January 15, 1861.
21. *Ibid.,* November 16, 1860.

22. *Weekly Herald,* November 15, 1860, quoting the *Eufaula Express,* n.d.
23. *Montgomery Weekly Advertiser,* December 26, 1860.
24. *Mobile Daily Advertiser,* December 9, 1860.
25. *Montgomery Daily Mail,* January 20, 1860.
26. Your Sister to James H. Hunter, January 3, 1861, Cobb-Hunter Papers, Southern Historical Collection, University of North Carolina.
27. *Montgomery Weekly Mail,* December 21, 1860.
28. *Montgomery Weekly Advertiser,* November 28, 1860.
29. *Ibid.,* January 9, 1861.
30. Richard B. Harwell, ed., *Kate: The Journal of a Confederate Nurse* (Baton Rouge, 1959), p. 34. Hereafter cited as *Kate.*
31. Virginia Clay-Clay-Clopton, *A Belle of the Fifties: Memoirs of Mrs. Clay, of Alabama* (New York, 1905), p. 151. Hereafter cited as *A Belle of the Fifties.*
32. [Augusta Jane Evans to Mrs. L. Virginia French, January 13, 1861] "Augusta J. Evans on Secession," *Alabama Historical Quarterly* 3 (Spring, 1941) : 65–67.
33. Ellen Noyes Jackson to Mary, February 19, 1861, Jefferson Franklin Jackson Papers, Alabama Department of Archives and History.
34. *Montgomery Weekly Mail,* February 16, 1861.
35. *Clark County Democrat* [Grove Hill], February 21, 1861, quoting the *Mobile Tribune,* n.d.
36. Elizsay Bell to brother, April 21, 1861, Executive Papers, Alabama Department of Archives and History.
37. *Mobile Daily Advertiser,* February 2, 1861, quoting the *Washington Constitution,* n.d.
38. Journal of Sarah G. Follansbee (MS in Alabama Department of Archives and History).
39. *Ibid.*
40. Elodie Todd to Nathaniel Dawson, July 4, 1861, Nathaniel Henry Rhodes Dawson Papers, Southern Historical Collection, University of North Carolina.
41. *Ibid.,* September 15, 1862.
42. *Montgomery Daily Mail,* February 16, 1861.
43. Mary A. H. Gay, *Life in Dixie During the War* (Atlanta, 1897), pp. 17–18. Hereafter cited as *Life in Dixie.*
44. Ellen N. Jackson to Mary, February 19, 1861, Jefferson Franklin Jackson Papers.
45. Louisiana Bradford to C. C. Clay, Jr. and Dr. Thomas Fearn, June 26, 1861, Clement Claiborne Clay Papers, Manuscript Division, Duke University.
46. Virginia Clay to Celeste Clay, July 14, 1861, in *ibid.*

Chapter 2

1. "The Patriotism of the Confederate Women as Seen by the Union Soldiers," *Reminiscences of Confederate Soldiers and Stories of the*

204   PARTNERS IN REBELLION

War, 1861–1865 (Typescript in Georgia State Archives, 1940) 2, p. 20.
2. *Montgomery Weekly Mail,* January 28, 1861.
3. Andrew Garrett to Virginia Clay, April 28, 1863, Clay Papers.
4. *Watchman* [Hayneville], March 8, 1861.
5. *Independent* [Gainesville], April 13, 1861.
6. "Major Sumpter Lea's Reply when Confederate Flag Presented to Marion Military Company by the Ladies of the Town, in April 61" (Typescript in Alabama Department of Archives and History).
7. *Southern Advertiser* [Troy], July 24, 1861.
8. Mildred B. Russell, *Lowndes Court House: A Chronicle of Hayneville An Alabama Black Belt Village, 1820–1900* (Montgomery, 1951), pp. 106–9. Hereafter cited as *Lowndes Court House.*
9. *Life in Dixie,* p. 17.
10. *Clarke County Democrat,* July 9, 1863, quoting the *Richmond Examiner,* n.d.
11. *Montgomery Daily Advertiser,* April 24, 1861, quoting the *Columbus Sun* [Georgia], n.d.
12. *Florence Gazette,* April 17, 1861.
13. *Daily Herald* [Montgomery], March 13, 1907, quoting the *Confederation* [Montgomery], June 23, 1861.
14. William G. Stevenson, *Thirteen Months in the Rebel Army* (New York, 1959), pp. 134–35.
15. *Selma Morning Reporter,* November 30, 1861.
16. *Ibid.,* January 13, 1862.
17. *Ibid.,* March 13, 1862.
18. Stevenson, *Thirteen Months in the Rebel Army,* pp. 134–35.
19. *Selma Evening Reporter,* August 10, 1863.
20. *Southern Advertiser,* March 26, 1861.
21. *Ibid.,* December 25, 1861.
22. *Ibid.,* April 8, 1863.
23. *Clarke County Democrat,* May 2, September 4, 1862.
24. *Mobile Advertiser and Register,* May 6, 1862.
25. *Selma Morning Reporter,* April 20, 1862.
26. *Mobile Register and Advertiser,* April 17, 1864.
27. *Independent,* May 7, June 22, 1861.
28. *Georgia Weekly Telegraph,* May 16, 1862, quoting the *Mobile Tribune,* n.d.
29. *Daily Herald,* March 13, 1907, quoting the *Alabama Beacon* [Greensboro], n.d.
30. Augusta J. Evans to Rachel Heutis, June 26, 1861 (Typescript in Alabama Department of Archives and History).
31. *Selma Morning Reporter,* March 3, 1862.
32. T. Harry Williams, *P. G. T. Beauregard: Napoleon in Gray* (Baton Rouge, 1954), p. 160.
33. *Ibid.,* p. 171.
34. Harwell, ed., *Kate,* pp. 28; 42.
35. *Ibid.,* pp. 171, 208–9.

36. Journal of Sarah Lowe (MS in Alabama Department of Archives and History).

37. *Southern Republic* [Opelika] May 7, 1861.

38. Harwell, ed., *Kate*, p. 183.

39. "Civil War Days in Huntsville: A Diary of Mrs. W. D. Chadick," *Alabama Historical Quarterly* 9 (Summer, 1947): 315. Hereafter cited as "Civil War Days in Huntsville."

40. Diaries of Martha Foster Crawford (MS in Manuscript Division, Duke University).

41. Minerva Abercrombie to son, May 28, 1862, Bolling Hall Papers, Alabama Department of Archives and History.

42. Fidler, *Augusta Evans Wilson*, pp. 87–88.

43. Harwell, ed., *Kate*, p. 260.

44. *Selma Morning Reporter,* March 8, 1862.

45. *Daily Herald,* March 13, 1907, quoting the *Confederation,* May 24, 1861.

46. Diary of Martha Jane Crossley, Rumph Family Manuscripts, Private Collection owned by Miss Effie Rumph, Perote, Alabama.

47. Harwell, ed., *Kate,* pp. 37, 259.

48. *Acts of the General Assembly of Alabama* (1864), p. 191.

Chapter 3

1. Newspaper Scrapbook of Belle Johnston, Alabama Department of Archives and History.

2. *Montgomery Daily Post,* July 30, 1861.

3. James B. Hall to Bolling Hall, August 9, 1862, Bolling Hall Papers, Alabama Department of Archives and History.

4. *Southern Republic,* February 11, 1862.

5. *Selma Morning Reporter,* December 30, 1861.

6. James B. Hall to Laura Hall, November 12, 1864, Bolling Hall Papers.

7. Diary of Aristide Hopkins (MS in Southern Historical Collection, University of North Carolina).

8. Julia Bate to Virginia Clay, March 8, 1862, Clay Papers.

9. George W. Gift to Ellen Shackleford, June 13, 1863, Ellen Shackleford Gift Papers, Southern Historical Collection, University of North Carolina.

10. Edward Y. McMorries, *History of the First Regiment Alabama Volunteer Infantry, C.S.A.* (Montgomery, 1904), pp. 33, 51–52. Hereafter cited as *History of First Regiment Alabama Volunteers.*

11. Bell I. Wiley, ed., *Sam R. Watkins, "Co. Aytch" Maury Grays First Tennessee Regiment or a Side Show of the Big Show* (Jackson, Tennessee, 1952), p. 144. Hereafter cited as *"Co. Aytch".*

12. William A. Sivley to Jane Sivley, June 19, 1864, Jane Sivley Letters, Southern Historical Collection, University of North Carolina.

13. Henry Clay Reynolds to wife, October 23, 1864, Henry Clay Reynolds Papers, Alabama Department of Archives and History.

14. Diary of James Wesley Riley (Typescript in Manuscript Division, Emory University).
15. Lucius W. Barber, *Army Memoirs of Lucius W. Barber Company "D", 15th Illinois Volunteer Infantry, May 24, 1861, to Sept. 30, 1865* (Chicago, 1894), pp. 142–43.
16. Lloyd Jenkin Jones, *An Artilleryman's Diary* (Madison, Wis., 1914), pp. 164, 183.
17. Jesse Hawes, *Cahaba: A Story of Captive Boys in Blue* (New York, 1888), pp 270–75.
18. *South Western Baptist* [Tuskegee], August 29, 1861.
19. Robert Tutwiler to Net and Kittie, April 28, 1863, Mrs. Thomas C. McCorvey Papers, Southern Historical Collection, University of North Carolina.
20. Hillary A. Herbert, "Grandfather Talks About His Life Under Two Flags: Reminiscences," (Typescript in Alabama Department of Archives and History), pp. 137–38. Hereafter cited as "Reminiscences."
21. Crenshaw Hall to Laura Hall, April 20, 1864, Bolling Hall Papers.
22. William C. Oates, *The War Between the Union and the Confederacy* . . . (New York, 1905), pp. 94–95.
23. Robert L. Bliss to mother, September 6, 1862, Robert L. Bliss Papers, Alabama Department of Archives and History.
24. Bell I. Wiley, *The Life of Johnny Reb: The Common Soldier in the Confederacy* (New York, 1943), p. 54.
25. "Letters of Major W. J. Mims," *Alabama Historical Quarterly* 18 (Winter, 1956): 211–12.
26. Mollie Mitchell to Margaret Brown, September 3, 1861, William Phineas Brown Papers, Alabama Department of Archives and History.
27. George W. Gift to Ellen Shackleford, January 25, 1863, Ellen Shackleford Gift Papers.
28. Thomas Hill Watts to Kate Watts, January 29, 1862, Thomas Hill Watts Papers, Alabama Department of Archives and History.
29. William B. Hall to Juliet Anderson, September 28, 1861, William B. Hall Papers.
30. Hugh Lawson Clay to Virginia Clay, December 26, 1862, Clement Claiborne Clay, Jr. Papers, War Research Division, Civil War Branch, National Archives, Washington, D. C.
31. Stephen R. Mallory to Virginia Clay, September 27, 1864, Clement Claiborne Clay, Jr. Papers, Manuscript Division, Duke University.
32. Hugh Lawson Clay to Virginia Clay, November 11, 1864 in *ibid.*
33. Toccoa Cozart, "What the Women of Montgomery Did," *Daily Herald* [Montgomery], March 13, 1907. Hereafter cited as "What the Women of Montgomery Did."
34. *Mobile Daily Advertiser,* March 31, 1861.
35. *Ibid.,* April 2, 1861.
36. *Mobile Weekly Advertiser,* December 19, 1862.
37. Robert L. Bliss to Arthur Bliss, March 22, 1863, Bliss Papers.

Chapter 4

1. Fidler, *Augusta Evans Wilson,* p. 95.
2. Alonzo B. Cohen to sister, January 12, 1861, Alonzo B. Cohen Papers, Alabama Department of Archives and History.
3. *Ibid.,* March 26, 1861.
4. Hugh L. Clay to Virginia Clay, June 4, 1861, Clay Papers.
5. Ruth K. Nuermberger, *The Clays of Alabama: A Planter-Lawyer-Politician Family* (Lexington, Kentucky, 1958), pp. 82–83. Hereafter cited as *The Clays of Alabama.*
6. Mrs. D. Giraud Wright, *A Southern Girl in '61: The War-Time Memories of a Confederate Senator's Daughter* (New York, 1905), p. 21. Hereafter cited as *A Southern Girl in '61.*
7. James B. Read to Virginia Clay, March 23, 1863, Clay Papers.
8. James Holt Clanton to Virginia Clay, February 24, 1863.
9. W. P. Barnes to Virginia Clay, February 24, 1863.
10. Euphradia Poeltnitz Johnson to Virginia Clay, June 8, 1861.
11. Clay-Clopton, *A Belle of the Fifties,* p. 204.
12. *Ibid.,* p. 202.
13. Nannie Yulee to Virginia Clay, December 9, 1863, Clay Papers.
14. Jefferson Davis to Virginia Clay, March 20, 1863.
15. *Ibid.,* August 31, 1864.
16. Hugh L. Clay to Virginia Clay, January 7, 1865.
17. Clay-Clopton, *A Belle of the Fifties,* p. 239.
18. Fidler, *Augusta Evans Wilson,* p. 117.
19. Augusta J. Evans to Jabez L. M. Curry, December 20, 1862, Jabez L. M. Curry Papers, Manuscript Division, Library of Congress, Washington, D. C.
20. Fidler, *Augusta Evans Wilson,* p. 92.
21. Augusta J. Evans to Curry, December 20, 1862, Curry Papers.
22. *Ibid.,* July 15, 1863, in *ibid.*
23. Augusta J. Evans to P. G. T. Beauregard, March 17, 1863, P. G. T. Beauregard Papers, Manuscript Division, Duke University.
24. Williams, *P. G. T. Beauregard,* p. 199.
25. Fidler, *Augusta Evans Wilson,* pp. 110–12.
26. Willis Brewer, *Alabama: Her History, Resources, War Record, and Public Men* (Montgomery, 1872), p. 423.
27. Journal of Sarah R. Espy.
28. Harwell, ed., *Kate,* p. 260.
29. Mrs. Dorian Hall to William B. Hall, February 12, 1862, William B. Hall Papers, Alabama Department of Archives and History.
30. *Mobile Weekly Advertiser and Register,* March 4, 1865.
31. *Ibid.*
32. Alice V. D. Pierrepont, comp., *Reuben Vaughn Kidd: Soldier of the Confederacy* (Petersburg, Virginia, 1947), p. 249.

33. Hugh Buckner Johnson, ed., "The Peel Confederate Letters," *Alabama Historical Quarterly* 8 (Spring, 1946): 89.
34. Horace M. Smith to wife, May 24, 1863, Horace Mortimer Smith Papers, Alabama Department of Archives and History.
35. Joel D. Murphree to Ursula Murphree, May 26, 1864, Private Collection owned by Halbert Wilkerson, Troy, Alabama.
36. *Ibid.*, August 15, 1864.
37. William C. McClellan to sister, October, 1864, Buchanan-McClelland Papers, Southern Historical Collection, University of North Carolina.
38. "Letters of Major W. J. Mims, C.S.A.," *Alabama Historical Quarterly* 3 (Summer, 1941): 210–11.
39. Phillips Fitzpatrick to Mary, June 22, 1862, Phillips Fitzpatrick Papers, Alabama Department of Archives and History.
40. Raphael Semmes to wife, January 4, 1863 (Typescript in *ibid.*).
41. Crenshaw Hall to Carrie, November 14, 1861, Bolling Hall Papers.
42. James A. Hall to Laura, October 22, 1863, in *ibid.*
43. Unidentified writer to mother, July 29, 1861 (Typescript in Alabama Department of Archives and History).
44. Harriet F. Ryan, ed., "The Letters of Harden Perkins Cochrane, 1862–64," *Alabama Review* 7, Part I (October, 1954): 286.
45. Clay-Clopton, *A Belle of the Fifties,* pp. 198–99.
46. "Confederate Letters of J. B. Cadenhead," *Alabama Historical Quarterly* 18 (Winter, 1956): 567.

Chapter 5

1. Diary of Martha Jane Crossley.
2. "List of Ladies' Aid Associations in Alabama, January 1, 1862," Executive Papers, Alabama Department of Archives and History.
3. *Montgomery Daily Post,* May 4, 1861.
4. Caroline Hausman to Governor John Gill Shorter [October, 1862], Executive Papers.
5. Harwell, ed., *Kate,* p. 85.
6. *South Western Baptist* [Tuskegee], August 8, 1861.
7. Caroline Hausman to Governor John Gill Shorter [October, 1862], Executive Papers.
8. *South Western Baptist,* July 25, 1861.
9. Walter M. Jackson, *Story of Selma* (Birmingham, 1954), p. 210.
10. *Southern Republic,* April 27, 1861.
11. *Ibid.,* July 20, 1861.
12. Annie Strudwick Diary and Letters, Southern Historical Collection, University of North Carolina.
13. Fannie A. Beers, *Memories: A Record of Personal Experiences and Adventures During Four Years of War* (Philadelphia, 1889), p. 54. Hereafter cited as Beers, *Memories.*
14. Mary Love Fleming, "Dale County and Its People During the Civil War," *Alabama Historical Quarterly* 19 (Spring, 1957): 90–91.

15. Diary of Martha Jane Crossley.
16. Adelaide deVendel Chaudron to Governor A. B. Moore, August 26, 1861, Executive Papers, Alabama Department of Archives and History.
17. "Proclamation Book A, 1860–1881, August 5, 1861," in *ibid.*
18. *Alabama Beacon* [Greensboro], August 9, 1862.
19. Caroline Hausman to Governor John Gill Shorter [October, 1862], Executive Papers.
20. Report of the Military Aid Society of Mobile, Statement of Work from May 4, 1861 to November 1, 1862, in *ibid.*
21. Margaret Burson to Shorter, October 22, 1862, in *ibid.*
22. *Southern Republic,* December 21, 1861.
23. *Selma Morning Reporter,* May 10, 12, 1862.
24. *Ibid.,* June 1, 1861.
25. Sam Wood to S. M. Wood [June, 1861]. (Typescript in S. M. Wood Papers, Alabama Department of Archives and History.)
26. *Mobile Advertiser and Register,* October 11, 1863.
27. *Selma Morning Reporter,* February 24, 1863.
28. Fidler, *Augusta Evans Wilson,* p. 90.
29. *Mobile Daily Advertiser,* January 13, 1861.
30. *Montgomery Daily Post,* July 25, 1861.
31. *Selma Morning Reporter,* March 10, 1862.
32. *Ibid.,* April 10, 1862.
33. *Montgomery Daily Advertiser,* April 15, 1862.
34. *Selma Morning Reporter,* May 14, 1862.
35. *Ibid.,* May 16, 1862.
36. Report of the Military Aid Society of Mobile, Statement of Work from May 4, 1861 to November 1, 1862, Executive Papers.
37. Adelaide deVendel Chaudron to Governor John Gill Shorter, May 1, 1863.
38. Laura Pillard to Governor John Gill Shorter, September 16, 1862.
39. *Mobile Advertiser and Register,* January 10, 1863.
40. *Montgomery Daily Advertiser,* April 15, 1862.
41. *Mobile Daily Tribune,* May 6, 1861.
42. Mrs. A. J. Reese to Governor A. B. Moore, August 20, 1861, Executive Papers.
43. *South Western Baptist,* October 10, 1861.
44. George W. Hails to Mrs. B. S. Bibb, September 29, 1861, George W. Hails Papers, Alabama Department of Archives and History; H. F. Stickney to Governor John Gill Shorter, February 25, 1863, Executive Papers.
45. Adelaide deVendel Chaudron to Shorter, March 19, 1863.
46. Margaret Browne to William F. Browne, June 5, 1861, William P. Browne Papers, Alabama Department of Archives and History.
47. Governor A. B. Moore to Colonel W. R. Pickett, September 6, 1861, Alabama Quartermaster General's Report in *ibid.*
48. *Ibid.,* September 23, 1861.

49. *Ibid.,* December 3, 1861.
50. "Circular Letter of Governor John Gill Shorter, August 26, 1862," Executive Papers.
51. *Acts of the General Assembly of Alabama* (1861), pp. 232–34; (1862), pp. 113–14; (1864), p. 33.
52. *Jacksonville Republican,* February 13, 1864.
53. Emilie Donald to Governor John Gill Shorter, September 22, 1862, Executive Papers.
54. Rebecca Dennis to Governor John Gill Shorter, May 25, 1862.
55. *Ibid.,* June 28, 1862.
56. *Montgomery Daily Post,* October 3, 1861.

Chapter 6

1. George W. Adams, "Confederate Medicine," *Journal of Southern History* 6 (May, 1944) : 151.
2. Oscar H. Lipscomb, "The Administration of John Quinlan, Second Bishop of Mobile, 1859–1883" (unpublished M.A. thesis, Catholic University of America, 1959), p. 72. Hereafter cited as "The Administration of John Quinlan, Second Bishop of Mobile."
3. Mrs. C. E. Trueheart to Governor A. B. Moore, June 20, 1861, Executive Papers, Alabama Department of Archives and History.
4. Marielou A. Cory, *The Ladies' Memorial Association of Montgomery, Alabama: Its Origin and Organization* (Montgomery, n.d.), pp. 13–14.
5. Thomas M. Owen, *History of Alabama and Dictionary of Alabama Biography* (Chicago, 1921), 3: 144–45. Hereafter cited as *History of Alabama.*
6. *Montgomery Advertiser,* January 11, 1887.
7. *Anniston Hot Blast,* March 13, 1907.
8. Edward H. Moren to wife, January 20, 1862, Edward H. Moren Papers, Alabama Department of Archives and History.
9. *Anniston Hot Blast,* March 13, 1907.
10. S. H. Stout to Mary J. Bell, January 19, 1864, S. H. Stout Papers, Manuscript Division, Emory University.
11. *Acts of the General Assembly of Alabama* (1861), pp. 232–33; (1862), p. 63; (1863), p. 113.
12. *Anniston Hot Blast,* March 13, 1907.
13. *Ibid.*
14. *Montgomery Advertiser,* January 11, 1887.
15. R. L. Brodie to George W. Brent, December 26, 1864 (Typescript in Alabama Department of Archives and History).
16. Fidler, *Augusta Evans Wilson,* p. 91.
17. Ellen G. McCloud, "Cared for a Sick Soldier Boy," *Confederate Veteran* 3 (January, 1895) : 9.
18. Clay-Clopton, *A Belle of the Fifties,* pp. 207–8.

19. R. L. Brodie to George W. Brent, December 26, 1864 (Typescript in Alabama Department of Archives and History).
20. *South Western Baptist,* February 20, 1862.
21. Report of the Military Aid Society of Mobile, Statement of Work, May 4, 1861 to November 1, 1862, Executive Papers.
22. N. Weedon to Thomas M. Owen, February 17, 1911, Thomas Adory Owen Papers, Alabama Department of Archives and History.
23. *Independent,* April 19, 1862; *Selma Morning Reporter,* June 7, 1862.
24. Beers, *Memories,* pp. 60–61, 67.
25. Owen, *History of Alabama,* 2: 328–29; 3: 884.
26. C. J. Clark to Governor John Gill Shorter, December 24, 1861, Executive Papers.
27. Beers, *Memories,* pp. 34–35.
28. Hospital Record Book, 1861–1863, Juliet Opie Hopkins Papers, Alabama Department of Archives and History.
29. Lucille Griffith, "Mrs. Juliet Opie Hopkins and Alabama Military Hospitals," *Alabama Review* 6 (April, 1953): 117–18; Hospital Register Containing an Account of Effects of Soldiers from May 1, 1862–July 20, 1863, Hopkins Papers.
30. Thomas Cooper DeLeon, *Belles, Beaux, and Brains of the 60's* (New York, 1909), p. 384. Hereafter cited as *Belles, Beaux, and Brains of the 60's.*
31. *Acts of the General Assembly of Alabama* (1861), p. 181; Governor John Gill Shorter to Arthur Hopkins, December 14, 1861, Executive Papers.
32. H. H. Cunningham, *Doctors in Gray: The Confederate Medical Service* (Baton Rouge, 1958), pp. 38, 50–51.
33. Hospital Record Book, 1861–1863; Ledger Accounts with State of Alabama for Hospitals 1–2–3, Hopkins Papers.
34. Griffith, "Mrs. Juliet Opie Hopkins," p. 116.
35. George Jones to Opie Hopkins, September 1, 1861, Hopkins Papers.
36. Jabez L. M. Curry to Opie Hopkins, September 25, 1862, in *ibid.*
37. *Daily Herald* [Montgomery], March 13, 1907.
38. Harwell, ed., *Kate,* p. 285.
39. Owen, *History of Alabama* 3: 844.
40. DeLeon, *Belles, Beaux, and Brains of the 60's,* p. 384.
41. Harwell, ed., *Kate,* p. 14.
42. *O.R.* Ser. I, 4: 199–200.
43. Harwell, ed., *Kate,* pp. 218–21.
44. *Ibid.,* pp. 38–39, 65.
45. *Ibid.,* p. xviii.
46. Epitaph of Sallie Swope, Greenwood Cemetery, Tuscaloosa, Alabama.
47. William H. Sanders to Fannie, August 19, 1861, William H. Sanders Papers, Alabama Department of Archives and History.
48. Robert Tutwiler to Nettie, September 2, 1861, Mrs. Thomas C. McCorvey Papers, Southern Historical Collection, University of North Carolina.

49. *Independent,* August 30, 1862, quoting the *Eutaw Whig,* n.d.
50. John William Jones, *Christ in the Camp: or, Religion in Lee's Army* (Richmond, 1888), p. 199.
51. J. V. Wright to Governor Thomas Hill Watts, February 16, 1865, Executive Papers.
52. Quoted in Lipscomb, "The Administration of John Quinlan, Second Bishop of Mobile," p. 74.
53. *Ibid.,* p. 75.
54. *Ibid.,* pp. 77–78.
55. *Ibid.,* p. 92.

Chapter 7

1. Ella Storrs Christian, "The Days That Are No More," *Alabama Historical Quarterly* 15, Part II (Spring, 1953) : 137.
2. Diary of Martha Jane Crossley.
3. Susanna Clay to C. C. Clay, Jr., March 5, 1862, Clay Papers.
4. *Ibid.,* March 24, 1862; September 5, 1863; March 14, 1865.
5. Chadick, "Civil War Days in Huntsville," pp. 226, 286.
6. Mary Fitzpatrick to husband [1861], Phillips Fitzpatrick Papers, Alabama Department of Archives and History.
7. Jane D. Brasfield to Governor John Gill Shorter, November 18, 1862, Executive Papers, in *ibid.*
8. Addie Harris to Governor John Gill Shorter, October 16, 1862; Mrs. A. S. McCain to Governor John Gill Shorter, October 5, 1862.
9. Christian, "The Days That Are No More," p. 348.
10. Parthenia A. Hague, *A Blockaded Family: Life in Southern Alabama During the Civil War* (Boston, 1888), pp. 32–33.
11. Fleming, "Dale County and Its People During the Civil War," pp. 97–100.
12. *Selma Morning Reporter,* December 30, 1862.
13. Harwell, ed., *Kate,* pp. 248–49.
14. *South Western Baptist,* April 21, 1862.
15. Jackson, *Story of Selma,* 198–99.
16. Thomas P. Clinton, "The Military Operations of General John T. Croxton in West Alabama, 1865," *Transactions of the Alabama Historical Society* 4, Part III (1899) : 449.
17. *Alabama Reporter* [Talladega], June 5, 1862.
18. *Selma Morning Reporter,* July 1, 1862.
19. *Selma Sentinel,* October 1, 1863, quoted in Jackson, *Story of Selma,* pp. 199–200.
20. *Ibid.*
21. W. Stanley Hoole, ed., "The Diary of Dr. Basil Manly, 1858–1867," *Alabama Review* 4, Part IV (January, 1962) : 64–65.
22. Wiley, ed. *"Co. Aytch,"* p. 180.

23. Albert T. Goodlow, *Confederate Echoes: A Voice from the South in the Days of Secession and the Southern Confederacy* (Nashville, 1907), pp. 170–71.
24. Diary of Martha Jane Crossley.
25. Fleming, "Dale County and Its People During the Civil War," pp. 84–85.
26. Nannie Rayburn to S. K. Rayburn, October 27, 1861, S. K. Rayburn Papers, Alabama Department of Archives and History.
27. *Independent,* June 18, 1861.
28. Edward H. Moren to Fannie, June 5, 1862, Moren Papers, Alabama Department of Archives and History.
29. Laurence M. Jones to Governor John Gill Shorter, March 17, 1862, Executive Papers, in *ibid.*
30. Lucreesy Simmons to Governor John Gill Shorter, July 17, 1862.
31. Mary Braswell to Governor John Gill Shorter, August 10, 1862.
32. Emily H. Hewlett to Governor John Gill Shorter, August 13, 1862.
33. Sarah A. Driggers to Governor John Gill Shorter, June 18, 1862.
34. Petition of Citizens of County Line [Monroe County], August 20, 1864, "Application for Exemption from Service in the Army," in *ibid.*
35. Petition of Citizens of Pine Grove [Coosa County], October 3, 1862, in *ibid.*
36. *O.R.,* Ser. I, 32: 764–765.
37. *Ibid.,* 52: 667.
38. *Selma Morning Reporter,* May 31, 1862.
39. *Ibid.,* September 27, 1862.
40. S. K. Rayburn to Governor John Gill Shorter, July 10, 1862; unidentified lady to Governor John Gill Shorter, January 19, 1863, Executive Papers.
41. J. A. Sullivan to Governor Thomas Hill Watts, February 28, 1864, in *ibid.*
42. *Mobile Advertiser and Register,* October 1, 1863, quoting the *New Orleans Era,* September 20, 1863.
43. *Acts of the General Assembly of Alabama* (1862), pp. 26–29; (1863), pp. 5–7, 58–61.
44. Charlotte R. Mitchell and Clyde E. Wilson, comps., "The Support of Indigent Families of Alabama Soldiers' Families Serving in the C.S.A., 1861–1865," Works Progress Administration, Historical Records Survey, 1937 (Typescript in Alabama Department of Archives and History).
45. *Acts of the General Assembly of Alabama* (1861), p. 81; (1863), pp. 84–85.
46. *Ibid.,* (1862), pp. 49, 59–61.
47. Provost Marshall General Report, 1863, Department of the Cumberland, 26: 212, War Records Division, Civil War Branch, National Archives.
48. Chadick, "Civil War Days in Huntsville," pp. 275–76.

Chapter 8

1. Ben Ames Williams, ed., Mary Boykin Chesnut, *A Diary from Dixie* (Boston, 1949), p. 287. Hereafter cited as *A Diary from Dixie*.
2. Kate H. Morrissette, "Social Life in the First Confederate Capital," *Daily Herald* [Montgomery], March 13, 1907. Hereafter cited as "Social Life in the First Confederate Capital."
3. Journal of Sarah C. Follansbee.
4. Frank E. Bestor to sister, May 21, 1863, Lida Bestor Robertson Papers, Alabama Department of Archives and History.
5. Celeste Clay to Virginia Clay, March, 1863, Clay Papers, Manuscript Division, Duke University.
6. Mary Russell to Samuel S. Parker, August 6, 1861, Mary Russell Parker Papers, Alabama Department of Archives and History.
7. Thomas B. Hall to Bolling Hall, Jr., June 15, 1863, Bolling Hall Papers, in *ibid.*
8. John H. Parrish to Dr. Sereno Watson, February 9, 1863, Henry Watson, Jr. Papers, Duke University.
9. Chesnut, *A Diary from Dixie*, p. 14.
10. Diary of Mary Mitchell Williamson (Typescript in Alabama Department of Archives and History).
11. Mary F. Clay to Virginia Clay, May 31, 1863, Clay Papers.
12. *Mobile Advertiser and Register*, May 3, 1864.
13. Hoole, ed., "The Diary of Dr. Basil Manly, 1858–1867," pp. 65–66.
14. Chadick, "Civil War Days in Huntsville," p. 247.
15. *Montgomery Daily Post*, June 28, 1861.
16. *Ibid.*, September 24, 1861.
17. *South Western Baptist*, August 1, 1861.
18. *Independent*, January 14, 1862.
19. *Selma Morning Reporter*, October 7, 11, 1861.
20. *Southern Advertiser* [Troy], January 1, 1862.
21. Mrs. E. L. Armstrong *et al.*, to Governor John Gill Shorter, November 15, 1862, Executive Papers.
22. Governor John Gill Shorter to James W. Taylor, March 1, 1862, in *ibid.*
23. *Southern Republic*, June 15, 1861.
24. *Mobile Advertiser and Register*, May 12, 13, 1864.
25. *Independent*, June 11, 25, 1864.
26. Thomas C. DeLeon, *Four Years in Rebel Capitals: An Inside View of Life in the Southern Confederacy from Birth to Death. . . .* (Mobile, 1892), p. 40.
27. Chesnut, *A Diary from Dixie*, p. 13.
28. *Ibid.*, pp. 6, 15, 50.
29. DeLeon, *Belles, Beaux, and Brains of the 60's*, p. 51.
30. Morrissette, "Social Life in the First Confederate Capital."
31. Fitzgerald Ross, *A Visit to the Cities and Camps of the Confederate States* (Edinburgh, 1865), pp. 240–43.

32. *Mobile Advertiser and Register,* January 10, 1863.

33. [Mrs. Dorian Hall] to William B. Hall, February 12, 1862, William B. Hall Papers, Alabama Department of Archives and History.

34. DeLeon, *Belles, Beaux, and Brains of the '60's,* pp. 182–85.

35. *Ibid.,* 186–90.

36. New York *Herald,* February 7, 1904, quoted in Mrs. Roger A. Pryor, *Reminiscences of Peace and War* (New York, 1904), p. 81.

37. Chesnut, *A Diary from Dixie,* pp. 368–69.

38. Quoted in Nuermberger, *The Clays of Alabama,* p. 220.

39. Thomas C. Irby to C. C. Clay, Jr., March 30, 1861, Clay Papers.

40. DeLeon, *Belles, Beaux, and Brains of the '60's,* 106–7.

41. Frank E. Vandiver, ed., *The Civil War Diary of General Josiah H. Gorgas* (University, Alabama, 1947), pp. 25, 52.

42. Mary E. Massey, *Refugee Life in the Confederacy* (Baton Rouge, 1964), pp. 280–82.

43. Elizabeth Avery Meriwether, *Recollection of 92 Years, 1824–1916* (Nashville, 1958), pp. 113–14.

44. *Ibid.,* pp. 122–24.

45. *Ibid.,* p. 127.

46. Diary of Frances W. Wallace (MS in Southern Historical Collection, University of North Carolina).

Chapter 9

1. Rebecca Thomas Bayless, "Yankee Raids on the South Side of the Tennessee," *Montgomery Advertiser,* May 3, 1908.

2. Walter L. Fleming, *Civil War and Reconstruction in Alabama* (New York, 1905), p. 62.

3. *O.R.,* Ser. I, 10:111.

4. Harvey S. Ford, ed., *John Beatty, The Citizen Soldier: or, Memoirs of a Volunteer* (New York, 1946), pp. 112–13. Hereafter cited as *The Citizen Soldier.*

5. "Letter from Huntsville, Yankeeville, Alabama, April 22, 1862," Newspaper Scrapbook of Mary J. Solomon, Manuscript Division, Duke University.

6. Bettie Burrleson to Jane Sivley, October 20, 1862, Sivley Papers, Southern Historical Collection.

7. *Selma Morning Reporter,* November 14, 1862.

8. Clay-Clopton, *A Belle of the Fifties,* p. 181.

9. Susanna Clay to C. C. Clay, Jr., July 22, 1862; M. Woolton to Virginia Clay, May 16, 1862, Clay Papers.

10. *O.R.,* Ser. I, 16:352.

11. Susanna Clay to C. C. Clay, Jr., September 5, 1863, Clay Papers.

12. Clay-Clopton, *A Belle of the Fifties,* p. 182.

13. Lila Greet, "Personal Reminiscences of Civil War Times Here," *Mercury Banner* [Huntsville], May 9, 1911.

14. Susanna Clay to C. C. Clay, Jr., March 6, 1862, Clay Papers.

15. John W. Clay to C. C. Clay, Jr., May 15, 1862, in *ibid.*
16. Newspaper Scrapbook of Mary J. Solomon.
17. Alberta C. Taylor, "Account of the Women of Huntsville," *Montgomery Advertiser,* April 26, 1908; Chadick, "Civil War Days in Huntsville," p. 209.
18. Chadick, "Civil War Days in Huntsville," p. 321.
19. *Ibid.,* pp. 226, 237, 263.
20. *Ibid.,* pp. 235–37.
21. *Ibid.,* pp. 267, 278, 306, 311.
22. Fleming, *Civil War and Reconstruction in Alabama,* p. 63; *Southern Advertiser* [Troy], August 6, 1862.
23. Mrs. E. A. O'Neal to husband, April 23, June 5, 1863, Edward Asbury O'Neal Papers, Southern Historical Collection, University of North Carolina.
24. Greet, "Personal Reminiscences of Civil War Times Here."
25. Diary of Daniel Coleman (MS in Southern Historical Collection, University of North Carolina).
26. Diary of J. B. Moore (Typescript in Alabama Department of Archives and History).
27. Newton Davis to wife, November 3, 1863, Newton Davis Papers, in *ibid.*
28. *O.R.,* Ser. I, 32:746–47; see also, Bessie Martin, *Desertion of Alabama Troops from the Confederate Army: A Study in Sectionalism* (New York, 1932), pp. 153–54.
29. Thomas C. Dunlap to Governor Thomas Hill Watts, April 17, 1864, Executive Papers.
30. Bush Jones to Governor John Gill Shorter, July 16, 1862, in *ibid.*
31. *New York Weekly Tribune,* March 14, 1863.
32. E. C. Betts to Governor Thomas Hill Watts, February 8, 1864, Executive Papers.
33. Chadick, "Civil War Days in Huntsville," pp. 213–14.
34. *O.R.,* Ser. I, 39:342.
35. *Ibid.,* 41:889.
36. *Ibid,.* 45:381.
37. Greet, "Personal Reminiscences of Civil War Times Here."
38. John A. Wyeth, *That Devil Forrest: Life of General Nathan Bedford Forrest* (New York, 1959), p. 190.
39. *Acts of the General Assembly of Alabama* (1863), pp. 213–14; (1899), p. 119.
40. *O.R.,* Ser. I, 49:426.
41. Diary of Mary Mitchell Williamson.
42. Ella Smith to Bessie [April], 1865, Washington M. Smith Papers, Manuscript Division, Duke University.
43. Christian, "The Ways That Are No More" (Spring, 1953), Part II, pp. 142–43.
44. Sarah Ellen Phillips, "Reminiscences Concerning Wilson's Raid in

Selma, 1865" (Typescript in Alabama Department of Archives and History).

45. Russell, *Lowndes Court House,* pp. 122–23.
46. Diary of Rev. Francis Hanson (Typescript in Southern Historical Collection, University of North Carolina).
47. Journal of Sarah G. Follansbee.
48. Diary of Steven V. Shipman (Typescript in Alabama Department of Archives and History).
49. Journal of Sarah G. Follansbee.
50. Journal of Mary D. Waring (Typescript in Southern Historical Collection).
51. Eliza Kendrick Walker, "Other Days: An Account of Plantation Life on Chunnennuggee Ridge Before the War Between the States," *Alabama Historical Quarterly* 5 Part II (Spring, 1943) : 209.
52. Ford, ed., *The Citizen Soldier,* p. 113.
53. Chadick, "Civil War Days in Huntsville," pp. 233, 238.
54. Tillie Houston to Mary C. Dalton, October 11, 1862, Mary Hunter Kennedy Papers, Southern Historical Collection.
55. Russell, *Lowndes Court House,* pp. 172–73.
56. B. A. Botkin, ed., *Lay My Burden Down: A Folk History of Slavery* (Chicago, 1946), pp. 206–7.

Chapter 10

1. Bell I. Wiley, *The Road to Appomattox* (Memphis, 1956), p. 73.
2. Journal of Sarah R. Espy.
3. Jesse Webb to James D. Webb, July 17, 1861, Walton Family Papers, Southern Historical Collection, University of North Carolina.
4. Martha Shorter to Virginia Clay, December 9, 1861, Clay Papers.
5. Diary of Mary Mitchell Williamson.
6. Beers, *Memories,* pp. 52–54.
7. Diary of Martha Jane Crossley.
8. McMorries, *History of the First Regiment Alabama Volunteers,* pp. 113–14.
9. Diary of Mary Mitchell Williamson.
10. Mrs. S. C. Cain to sister, July 19, 1863, Martha M. Jones Letters and Papers, Manuscript Division, Duke University.
11. Ruby Browne to mother, August 11, 1861, William Pheneas Browne Papers, Alabama Department of Archives and History.
12. Harwell, ed., *Kate,* p. 153.
13. "Civil War Days in Huntsville," p. 298.
14. Bayless, "Yankee Raids on the South Side of the Tennessee."
15. Mrs. E. A. O'Neal to husband, June 5, 1863, Edward Asbury O'Neal Papers.
16. Quoted in Nina Leftwich, *Two Hundred Years at Muscle Shoals . . .* Birmingham, 1935), p. 211.

218   PARTNERS IN REBELLION

17. *Ibid.*
18. Clay-Clopton, *A Belle of the Fifties,* pp. 180–81.
19. Anne Easby-Smith, *William Russell Smith of Alabama: His Life and Works, Including the Entire Text of the Uses of Solitude* (Philadelphia, 1931), p. 146.
20. Mary Fitzpatrick to Phillips Fitzpatrick, June 28, June 30, 1862, Phillips Fitzpatrick Papers.
21. Wilhelmine Easby-Smith to William R. Smith, February 5, 1863, William Russell Smith Papers, Southern Historical Collection.
22. General W. S. Rosecrans Daily Summary Record, Department of the Cumberland, War Research Division, Civil War Branch, National Archives, Washington, D.C.
23. Journal of Sarah G. Follansbee.
24. Octavia Levert to J. L. M. Curry, March 18, 1863, Jabez L. M. Curry Papers, Manuscript Division, Library of Congress, Washington, D.C.
25. Quoted in Leftwich, *Two Hundred Years at Muscle Shoals,* pp. 210–11.
26. J. W. A. Sanford to mother, July 5, 1863, J. W. A. Sanford Papers, Alabama Department of Archives and History.
27. December 24, 1864.
28. *Montgomery Daily Advertiser,* March 3, 1865.
29. *Mobile Weekly Advertiser and Register,* March 4, 1865.
30. Diaries of Martha F. Crawford (MSS in Manuscript Division, Duke University).
31. "Civil War Days in Huntsville," pp. 322–23.
32. Quoted in Harwell, ed., *Kate,* pp. 306–7.
33. *Ibid.,* 307.
34. Laura Harris Craighead, *History of the Alabama Federation of Women's Clubs* (Montgomery, 1936), pp. 14–15.
35. Lee N. Allen, "The Woman Suffrage Movement in Alabama, 1910–1920," *Alabama Review* 11 (April, 1958):98–99.

Bibliography

I
Primary Sources

A. Manuscripts

Pierre Gustave Toutant Beauregard Papers. Manuscript Division, Duke University.

Robert L. Bliss Papers. Alabama Department of Archives and History.

James Locke Boardman Papers. Manuscript Division, Duke University.

R. L. Brodie to George W. Brent, December 26, 1864. Typescript letter in Alabama Department of Archives and History.

William Phineas Browne Papers. Alabama Department of Archives and History.

Buchanan-McClellan Papers, Southern Historical Collection, University of North Carolina.

Clement Claiborne Clay Papers. Manuscript Division, Duke University.

Clement Claiborne Clay Papers. War Research Division, Civil War Branch, National Archives.

Cobb-Hunter Papers. Southern Historical Collection, University of North Carolina.

Alonzo B. Cohen Papers. Alabama Department of Archives and History.

Diary of Daniel Coleman. Southern Historical Collection, University of North Carolina.

Diaries of Martha Foster Crawford, Manuscript Division, Duke University.

Diary of Martha Jane Crossley. Rumph Family Manuscripts, Private Collection owned by Effie Rumph, Perote, Alabama.

Jabez Lamar Monroe Curry Papers. Manuscript Division, Library of Congress.

Newton Davis Papers. Alabama Department of Archives and History.

Nathaniel Henry Rhodes Dawson Papers. Southern Historical Collection, University of North Carolina.

"As Wesley Tells It: Excerpts from the Diary of Wesley M. DeHaven: A Soldier in the Union Army." Typescript in Georgia State Archives.

George Phifer Erwin Papers. Southern Historical Collection, University of North Carolina.

Journal of Sarah R. Espy. Typescript in Alabama Department of Archives and History.

Augusta Jane Evans to Mrs. Rachael Heutis, June 26, 1861. Typescript in Alabama Department of Archives and History.

Phillips Fitzpatrick Papers. Alabama Department of Archives and History.

Journal of Sarah G. Follansbee. Alabama Department of Archives and History.

George W. Hails Papers. Alabama Department of Archives and History.

Bolling Hall Papers. Alabama Department of Archives and History.

William B. Hall Papers. Alabama Department of Archives and History.

Diary of Rev. Francis Hanson. Typescript in Southern Historical Collection, University of North Carolina.

Arthur F. Harmon Papers. Alabama Department of Archives and History.

Hillary A. Herbert, "Grandfather Talks about His Life under Two Flags: Reminiscences." Typescript in Alabama Department of Archives and History.

Diary of Artistide Hopkins. Southern Historical Collection, University of North Carolina.

Juliet Ann [Opie] Hopkins Papers. Alabama Department of Archives and History.

Jefferson Franklin Jackson Papers, Alabama Department of Archives and History.

Newspaper Scrapbook of Belle Johnston. Alabama Department of Archives and History.

Martha M. Jones Papers and Letters, Manuscript Division, Duke University.

Mary Hunter Kennedy Papers. Southern Historical Collection, University of North Carolina.

"Major Sumpter Lea's Reply when Confederate Flag Presented to Marion Military Company by the Ladies of the Town, in April, 61." Typescript in Alabama Department of Archives and History.

Journal of Sarah Lowe. Alabama Department of Archives and History.

Mrs. Thomas C. McCorvey Papers. Southern Historical Collection, University of North Carolina.

Diary of J. B. Moore. Typescript in Alabama Department of Archives and History.

Edward H. Moren Papers. Alabama Department of Archives and History.

Joel Dyer Murphee Letters. Private Collection owned by Halbert Wilkerson, Troy, Alabama.

Edward Asbury O'Neal Papers. Southern Historical Collection, University of North Carolina.

Thomas McAdory Owen Papers. Alabama Department of Archives and History.

George W. Parsons Papers. Alabama Department of Archives and History.

"The Patriotism of the Confederate Women as Seen by the Union Soldiers: Reminiscences of Confederate Soldiers and Stories of the War, 1861–1865," 10 vol. Typescript in Georgia State Archives.

Ruby F. Ray, ed. "Letters and Diary of Lieut. Lavender R. Ray, 1861–1865." Typescript in Georgia State Archives.

Samuel K. Rayburn Papers. Alabama Department of Archives and History.

Henry Clay Reynolds Papers. Alabama Department of Archives and History.

Diary of James Wesley Riley. Typescript in Manuscript Division, Emory University.

Lida Bestor Robertson Papers. Alabama Department of Archives and History.

Mary Russell Papers. Alabama Department of Archives and History.

William H. Sanders Papers. Alabama Department of Archives and History.

J. W. A. Sanford Papers. Alabama Department of Archives and History.

Raphael Semmes Letters. Typescript in Alabama Department of Archives and History.

Ellen Shackelford Gift Papers. Southern Historical Collection, University of North Carolina.

Diary of Steven Vaughn Shipman. Typescript in Alabama Department of Archives and History.

Jane Sivley Letters. Southern Historical Collection, University of North Carolina.

Horace Mortimer Smith Papers. Alabama Department of Archives and History.

Washington M. Smith Papers. Manuscript Division, Duke University.

William Russell Smith Papers. Southern Historical Collection, University of North Carolina.

Scrapbook of Mary J. Soloman. Manuscript Division, Duke University.

Samuel H. Stout Papers. Manuscript Division, Emory University.

Annie Strudwick Diary and Letters. Microfilm in Southern Historical Collection, University of North Carolina.

Epitaph of Sallie Swope. Greenwood Cemetery, Tuscaloosa, Alabama.

Unsigned Letter, July 24, 1861. Typescript in Alabama Department of Archives and History.

"Diary of Charles Robert Walden of Talladega, Alabama 1st Company of Washington Artillery, Sept. 1863–May, 1864." Typescript in Georgia State Archives.

Diary of Charles Robert Walden. Alabama Department of Archives and History.

Diary of Frances Woolfolk Wallace. Southern Historical Collection, University of North Carolina.

Walton Family Papers. Southern Historical Collection, University of North Carolina.

Journal of Mary D. Waring. Typescript in Southern Historical Collection, University of North Carolina.

Henry Watson, Jr. Papers. Manuscript Division, Duke University.

Thomas Hill Watts Papers. Alabama Department of Archives and History.

Diary of Mary Mitchell Williamson. Typescript in Alabama Department of Archives and History.

August Evans Wilson Papers. Alabama Department of Archives and History.

Sam M. Wood Papers. Alabama Department of Archives and History.

B. Published Correspondence, Diaries, Memoirs, Reminiscences

Andrews, Eliza Frances. *The War Time Journal of a Georgia Girl.* New York: D. Appleton and Company, 1908.

Bayless, Rebecca Thompson. "Yankee Raids on the South Side of the Tennessee," *Montgomery Advertiser,* May 3, 1908.

Beers, Mrs. Fannie A. *Memories: A Record of Personal Experience and Adventure During the Four Years of War.* Philadelphia: J. B. Lippincott Company, 1889.

Botkin, B. A., ed. *Lay My Burden Down: A Folk History of Slavery.* Chicago: University of Chicago Press, 1946.

"Civil War Days in Huntsville: A Diary of Mrs. W. D. Chadick." *Alabama Historical Quarterly* 9 (1947).

Christian, Ella Storrs. "The Days That Are No More," *Alabama Historical Quarterly,* 14–15 (1951–1952).

Chesnut, Mary Boykin. *Diary from Dixie.* Boston: Houghton Mifflin Company, 1950.

Clay-Clopton, Virginia. *A Belle of the Fifties: Memoirs of Mrs. Clay, of Alabama, covering social and political life in Washington and the South, 1853–66: Put into narrative form by Ada Sterling.* New York: Doubleday, Page and Company, 1905.

"Confederate Letters of J. B. Cadenhead." *Alabama Historical Quarterly* 18 (1956).

Cozart, Toccoa. "What the Women of Montgomery Did." *Daily Herald* (Montgomery), March 13, 1907.

DeLeon, Thomas Cooper. *Belles, Beaux, and Brains of the 60's.* New York: G. W. Dillingham Company, 1909.

———. *Four Years in Rebel Capitals: An Inside View of Life in the Southern Confederacy, From Birth to Death: from original notes collected in the years 1861–1865.* Mobile: Gossip Printing Company, 1892.

"Augusta J. Evans on Secession." *Alabama Historical Quarterly* 3 (1941).

Fleming, Mary Love. "Dale County and Its People During the Civil War." *Alabama Historical Quarterly* 19 (1957).

Ford, Harvey S., ed. *John Beatty, The Citizen Soldier: or Memoirs of a Volunteer.* New York: W. W. Norton and Company, 1946.

Gay, Mary A. H. *Life in Dixie During the War.* Atlanta: Charles P. Byrd Company, 1897.

Goodlow, Albert T. *Confederate Echoes: A Voice from the South in the Days of Secession and the Southern Confederacy.* Nashville: Publishing House of the M. E. Church, South; Smith and Lower, 1907.

Greet, Lila. "Personal Reminiscences of Civil War Times Here." *Huntsville Mercury Banner,* May 9, 1911.

Hague, Parthenia Antoinette. *A Blockaded Family: Life in Southern Alabama During the Civil War.* Boston: Houghton Mifflin Company, 1888.

Harwell, Richard Barksdale, ed. *Kate: The Journal of a Confederate Nurse.* Baton Rouge: Louisiana State University Press, 1959.

Hawes, Jesse. *Cahaba: A Story of Captive Boys in Blue.* New York: Burr Printing House, 1888.

Hoole, W. Stanley, ed., "The Diary of Dr. Basil Manly, 1858–1867," *Alabama Review* 5 (1952).

Johnson, Hugh Buckner, ed., "The Peel Confederate Letters." *Alabama Historical Quarterly* 8 (1946).

Jones, Jenkin Lloyd. *An Artilleryman's Diary.* Madison, Wisconsin: Wisconsin Historical Commission, 1914.

Jones, John William. *Christ in the Camp: or, Religion in Lee's Army Supplemented by a Sketch of the Work in the Other Confederate Armies*. Richmond: B. D. Johnson and Company, 1888.

"Letters of Major W. J. Mims, C.S.A." *Alabama Historical Quarterly* 3 (1941).

McCord, Ellen G. "Cared for a Sick Soldier Boy." *Confederate Veteran* 3 (1895).

McMorries, Edward Y. *History of the First Regiment, Alabama Volunteer Infantry, C. S. A.* Montgomery: The Brown Company, 1904.

Meriwether, Elizabeth Avery. *Recollections of 92 Years, 1824–1916*. Nashville: The Tennessee Historical Commission, 1958.

Morrissette, Kate H. "Social Life in the First Confederate Capital." *Daily Herald* [Montgomery], March 13, 1907.

Phillips, Sarah Ellen. "Reminiscences Concerning Wilson's Raid in Selma, 1865." Typescript in Alabama Department of Archives and History.

Pierrepont, Alice V. D. *Reuben Vaughn Kidd: Soldier of the Confederacy*. Petersburg, Virginia: Published by the author, 1947.

Pryor, Mrs. Roger Atkinson. *Reminiscences of Peace and War*. New York: The MacMillan Company, 1904.

Ross, Fitzgerald. *A Visit to the Cities and Camps of the Confederate States*. Edinburgh: William Blackwood and Sons, 1865.

Ryan, Harriet Fitts, ed. "The Letters of Harden Perkins Cockrane, 1862–64." *Alabama Review*, 7–8 (1954–1955).

Stevenson, William G. *Thirteen Months in the Rebel Army*. New York: A. S. Barnes and Company, 1959.

Taylor, Alberta C. "What Some Women of Huntsville Did in Confederate Times." *Montgomery Advertiser,* April 26, 1908.

Vandiver, Frank E., ed. *The Civil War Diary of General Josiah H. Gorgas*. University, Alabama: University of Alabama Press, 1947.

Walker, Kendrick Eliza J. "Other Days: An Account of Plantation Life on Chunnennugee Ridge before the War Between the States." *Alabama Historical Quarterly* 3–5 (1941–1943).

Wheeler, Joseph. "Mrs. Arthur Hopkins: A Distinguished Philanthropic and Patriotic Woman." *Daily Herald* [Montgomery], March 13, 1907.

Wright, Mrs. D. Giraud. *A Southern Girl in '61: The War-Time Memories of a Confederate Senator's Daughter.* New York: Doubleday, Page, and Company, 1905.

C. Public Documents

1. General

Agriculture of the United States in 1860: Compiled from the original returns of the Eighth Census, under the direction of the Secretary of the Interior, by Joseph C. G. Kennedy, Superintendent of Census. Washington: Government Printing Office, 1864.

Cotterall, Helen Turncliff, ed. *Judicial Cases concerning American Slavery and the Negro.* Washington: Published by the Carnegie Institute of Washington, 3, 1932.

Manufactures of the United States in 1860: Compiled from the original returns of the Eighth Census, under the direction of the Secretary of the Interior, by Joseph C. G. Kennedy, Superintendent of Census. Washington: Government Printing Office, 1865.

Population of the United States in 1860: Compiled from the original returns of the Eighth Census, under the direction of the Secretary of Interior, by Joseph C. G. Kennedy, Superintendent of Census. Washington: Government Printing Office, 1864.

Provost Marshal's General Report, 1863. Department of the Cumberland, vol. 26. War Records Division, Civil War Branch, National Archives, Washington, D.C.

General W. S. Rosecrans Daily Summary Record. Department of the Cumberland, War Records Division, Civil War Branch, National Archives, Washington, D.C.

The War of the Rebellion: A Compilation of the Official Records of the Union and Confederate Armies. 130 vols. Washington: Government Printing Office, 1880–1902.

2. State

Acts of the General Assembly of Alabama, 1860–1865; 1899.

Alabama Quartermaster Generals' Reports, 1861–1863. Alabama Department of Archives and History, Montgomery, Alabama.

"Circular Letter, August 26, 1862." Executive Papers, Alabama Department of Archives and History.

Governors' Letter Books, 1860–1861. Executive Papers, Alabama Department of Archives and History.

Mitchell, Charlotte R. and Wilson, Clyde E., comps. "The Support of Indigent Families of Alabama Soldiers Serving the C.S.A. 1861–1865." Works Progress Administration, Historical Records Survey, 1937. Typescript in Alabama Department of Archives and History.

"Proclamation Book A, 1860–1861." Executive Papers, Alabama Department of Archives and History.

Reports of Mobile Military Aid Society to Governor John Gill Shorter, 1861–1863. Executive Papers, Aalabama Department of Archives and History.

D. Newspapers

Alabama Beacon, Greensboro, Alabama.
Alabama Reporter, Talladega, Alabama.
Anniston Hot Blast, Anniston, Alabama.
Clarke County Democrat, Grove Hill, Alabama.
Daily Herald, Montgomery, Alabama.
Florence Gazette, Florence, Alabama.
Huntsville Mercury Banner, Huntsville, Alabama.
Independent, Gainesville, Alabama.
Jacksonville Republican, Jacksonville, Alabama.
Mobile Advertiser and Register, Mobile, Alabama.
Mobile Daily Advertiser, Mobile, Alabama.
Mobile Register and Advertiser, Mobile, Alabama.
Mobile Tribune, Mobile, Alabama.
Mobile Weekly Advertiser and Register, Mobile, Alabama.
Montgomery Advertiser, Montgomery, Alabama.
Montgomery Daily Advertiser, Montgomery, Alabama.
Montgomery Daily Mail, Montgomery, Alabama.
Montgomery Daily Post, Montgomery, Alabama.
Montgomery Weekly Advertiser, Montgomery, Alabama.
Montgomery Weekly Mail, Montgomery, Alabama.
New York Weekly Tribune, New York, New York.
Selma Evening Reporter, Selma, Alabama.

Selma Morning Reporter, Selma, Alabama.
Southern Advertiser, Troy, Alabama.
Southern Republic, Opelika, Alabama.
South Western Baptist, Tuskegee, Alabama.
Watchman, Hayneville, Alabama.
Weekly Herald, Benton, Alabama.

II
Secondary Sources

A. Periodicals

Adams, George W. "Confederate Medicine." *Journal of Southern History* 6 (1940).
Allen, Lee N. "The Women Suffrage Movement in Alabama, 1910–1920." *Alabama Review* 11 (1958).
Clinton, Thomas P. "The Military Operations of General John T. Croxton in West Alabama, 1865." *Transactions of the Alabama Historical Society* 4 (1899).
Griffith, Lucille. "Mrs. Juliet Opie Hopkins and Alabama Military Hospitals." *Alabama Review* 6 (1953).
Venable, Austin L. "William L. Yancey's Transition from Unionism to States Rights." *Journal of Southern History* 10 (1944).

B. Special Monographs

Andrews, Matthew Page, ed. *The Women of the South in War Times.* Baltimore: The Norman Remington Company, 1920.
Barber, Lucius W. *Army Memoirs of Lucius W. Barber Company "D" 15 Illinois Volunteer Infantry.* Chicago: The J. M. W. Jones Stationary and Printing Company, 1894.
Bill, Alfred Hoyt. *The Beleaguered City: Richmond 1861–1865.* New York: Alfred A. Knopf, 1946.
Boyd, Minnie Clare. *Alabama in the Fifties: A Social Study.* New York: Columbia University Press, 1931.
Brewer, Willis. *Alabama: Her History, Resources, War Record, and Public Men.* Montgomery: Barrett and Brown, 1872.
Cory, Marielou Armstrong. *The Ladies' Memorial Association of Montgomery, Alabama: Its Origin and Organization, 1860–1870.* Montgomery: Alabama Printing Company, n.d.

Coulter, E. Merton. *The Confederate States of America, 1861–1865*. Baton Rouge: Louisiana State University Press, 1950.

Craighead, Laura Harris. *History of the Alabama Federation of Women's Clubs*. Montgomery: The Paragon Press, 1936.

Cunningham, H. H. *Doctors in Gray: The Confederate Medical Service*. Baton Rouge: Louisiana State University Press, 1958.

Dawson, Francis Warrington. *Our Women in the War*. Charleston: Walker, Evans and Cogwell, 1887.

DuBose, John Witherspoon. *The Life and Times of William Lowndes Yancey*. Birmingham: Roberts and Son, 1892.

Dyer, Frederick H., comp. *A Compendium of the War of the Rebellion*. 3 vols. New York: Thomas Yoseloff, 1959.

Fidler, William P. *Augusta Evans Wilson, 1835–1900: A Biography*. University, Alabama: University of Alabama Press, 1951.

Fleming, Walter L. *Civil War and Reconstruction in Alabama*. New York: Columbia University Press, 1905.

Garrett, William. *Reminiscences of Public Men in Alabama, for Thirty Years*. Atlanta: Plantation Publishing Company's Press, 1872.

Jackson, Walter M., *The Story of Selma*. Birmingham: The Birmingham Printing Company, 1954.

Jones, Katharine M. *Heroines of Dixie: Confederate Women Tell Their Story of the War*. New York: The Bobbs-Merrill Company, Inc., 1955.

Leftwich, Nina. *Two Hundred Years at Muscle Shoals: Being An Authentic History of Colbert County 1700–1900 with special emphasis on the stirring events of the early times*. Birmingham: Published by the author, 1935.

McMillan, Malcolm Cook, ed. *The Alabama Confederate Reader*. University, Alabama: University of Alabama Press, 1963.

Martin, Bessie. *Desertion of Alabama Troops from the Confederate Army: A Study in Sectionalism*. New York: Columbia University Press, 1932.

Massey, Mary Elizabeth. *Bonnet Brigades*. New York: Alfred A. Knopf, 1966.

———. *Ersatz in the Confederacy*. Columbia: University of South Carolina Press, 1952.

————. *Refugee Life in the Confederacy*. Baton Rouge: Louisiana State University Press, 1964.

Nuermberger, Ruth Ketring. *The Clays of Alabama: A Planter-Lawyer-Politician Family*. Lexington: University of Kentucky Press, 1958.

Oates, William C. *The War Between the Union and the Confederacy and Its Lost Opportunities with a history of the 15th Alabama Regiment and the forty-eight battles in which it was engaged*. . . . New York: The Neale Publishing Company, 1905.

Osterweis, Rollin G. *Romanticism and Nationalism in the Old South*. New Haven: Yale University Press, 1949.

Owen, Marie Bankhead. *The Story of Alabama: A History of the State*. 5 vols. New York: Lewis Historical Publishing Company, 1949.

Owen, Thomas M. *History of Alabama and Dictionary of Alabama Biography*. 4 vols. Chicago: S. J. Clark Publishing Company, 1921.

Ramsdell, Charles W. *Behind the Lines in the Southern Confederacy*. Baton Rouge: Louisiana State University Press, 1944.

Russell, Mildred Brewer. *Lowndes Court House: A Chronicle of Hayneville and Alabama Black Belt Village*. Montgomery: The Paragon Press, 1951.

Simkins, Francis B. and Patton, James M. *The Women of the Confederacy*. Richmond: Garrett and Massie, Inc., 1936.

Easby-Smith, Anne. *William Russell Smith of Alabama: His Life and Works Including the Entire Text of the Uses of Solitude*. Philadelphia: The Dolphin Press, 1931.

Wiley, Bell I., ed. *Sam R. Watkins, "Co. Aytch" Maury Grays First Tennessee Regiment of a Side Show of the Big Show*. Jackson, Tennessee: McCowat-Mercer Press, 1952.

————. *The Plain People of the Confederacy*. Baton Rouge: Louisiana State University Press, 1944.

————. *The Road to Appomattox*. Memphis: Memphis State College Press, 1956.

Williams, T. Harry. *P. G. T. Beauregard: Napoleon in Gray*. Baton Rouge: Louisiana State University Press, 1954.

Wooster, Ralph A. *The Secession Conventions of the South*. Princeton: Princeton University Press, 1962.

Wyeth, John Allen. *That Devil Forrest: Life of General Nathan Bedford Forrest.* New York: Harper and Brothers, 1959.

III

Theses and Dissertations

Lipscomb, Oscar H., "The Administration of John Quinlan, Second Bishop of Mobile, 1859–1883." Unpublished M. A. thesis, Catholic University of America, 1959.

Index

233